V.

TONY HARRISON

V.

WITHDRAWN

BLOODAXE BOOKS

ISBN: 978 0 906427 97 2

First published 1985 by
Bloodaxe Books Ltd,
Highgreen,
Tarset,
Northumberland NE48 1RP.

Second edition 1989
Reprinted 1991, 1994, 2000, 2008

www.bloodaxebooks.com
For further information about Bloodaxe titles
please visit our website or write to
the above address for a catalogue.

Bloodaxe Books Ltd acknowledges
the financial assistance of
Arts Council England, North East.

Typesetting by True North, Newcastle upon Tyne.

Cover printing: J. Thomson Colour Printers Ltd, Glasgow.

Printed in Great Britain by
Cromwell Press Ltd, Trowbridge, Wiltshire.

'My father still reads the dictionary every day. He says your life depends on your power to master words.'

ARTHUR SCARGILL
Sunday Times, 10 January 1982

Next millennium you'll have to search quite hard
to find my slab behind the family dead,
butcher, publican, and baker, now me, bard
adding poetry to their beef, beer and bread.

With Byron three graves on I'll not go short
of company, and Wordsworth's opposite.
That's two peers already, of a sort,
and we'll all be thrown together if the pit,

whose galleries once ran beneath this plot,
causes the distinguished dead to drop
into the rabblement of bone and rot,
shored slack, crushed shale, smashed prop.

Wordsworth built church organs, Byron tanned
luggage cowhide in the age of steam,
and knew their place of rest before the land
caves in on the lowest worked-out seam.

This graveyard on the brink of Beeston Hill's
the place I may well rest if there's a spot
under the rose roots and the daffodils
by which dad dignified the family plot.

If buried ashes saw then I'd survey
the places I learned Latin, and learned Greek,
and left, the ground where Leeds United play
but disappoint their fans week after week,

which makes them lose their sense of self-esteem
and taking a short cut home through these graves here
they reassert the glory of their team
by spraying words on tombstones, pissed on beer.

This graveyard stands above a worked-out pit.
Subsidence makes the obelisks all list.
One leaning left's marked FUCK, one right's marked SHIT
sprayed by some peeved supporter who was pissed.

Far-sighted for his family's future dead,
but for his wife, this banker's still alone
on his long obelisk, and doomed to head
a blackened dynasty of unclaimed stone,

now graffitied with a crude four-letter word.
His children and grandchildren went away
and never came back home to be interred,
so left a lot of space for skins to spray.

The language of this graveyard ranges from
a bit of Latin for a former Mayor
or those who laid their lives down at the Somme,
the hymnal fragments and the gilded prayer,

how people 'fell asleep in the Good Lord',
brief chisellable bits from the good book
and rhymes whatever length they could afford,
to CUNT, PISS, SHIT and (mostly) FUCK!

Or, more expansively, there's LEEDS v.
the opponent of last week, this week, or next,
and a repertoire of blunt four-letter curses
on the team or race that makes the sprayer vexed.

Then, pushed for time, or fleeing some observer,
dodging between tall family vaults and trees
like his team's best ever winger, dribbler, swerver,
fills every space he finds with versus Vs.

Vs sprayed on the run at such a lick,
the sprayer master of his flourished tool,
get short-armed on the left like that red tick
they never marked his work much with at school.

Half this skinhead's age but with approval
I helped whitewash a V on a brick wall.
No one clamoured in the press for its removal
or thought the sign, in wartime, rude at all.

These Vs are all the versuses of life
from LEEDS v. DERBY, Black/White
and (as I've known to my cost) man v. wife,
Communist v. Fascist, Left v. Right,

class v. class as bitter as before,
the unending violence of US and THEM,
personified in 1984
by Coal Board MacGregor and the NUM,

Hindu/Sikh, soul/body, heart v. mind,
East/West, male/female, and the ground
these fixtures are fought out on's Man, resigned
to hope from his future what his past never found.

The prospects for the present aren't too grand
when a swastika with NF (National Front)'s
sprayed on a grave, to which another hand
has added, in a reddish colour, CUNTS.

Which is, I grant, the word that springs to mind,
when going to clear the weeds and rubbish thrown
on the family plot by football fans, I find
UNITED graffitied on my parents' stone.

How many British graveyards now this May
are strewn with rubbish and choked up with weeds
since families and friends have gone away
for work or fuller lives, like me from Leeds?

When I first came here 40 years ago
with my dad to 'see my grandma' I was 7.
I helped dad with the flowers. He let me know
she'd gone to join my grandad up in Heaven.

My dad who came each week to bring fresh flowers
came home with clay stains on his trouser knees.
Since my parents' deaths I've spent 2 hours
made up of odd 10 minutes such as these.

Flying visits once or twice a year,
and though I'm horrified just who's to blame
that I find instead of flowers cans of beer
and more than one grave sprayed with some skin's name?

Where there were flower urns and troughs of water
and mesh receptacles for withered flowers
are the HARP tins of some skinhead Leeds supporter.
It isn't all his fault though. Much is ours.

5 kids, with one in goal, play 2-a-side.
When the ball bangs on the hawthorn that's one post
and petals fall they hum *Here Comes the Bride*
though not so loud they'd want to rouse a ghost.

They boot the ball on purpose at the trunk
and make the tree shed showers of shrivelled may.
I look at this word graffitied by some drunk
and I'm in half a mind to let it stay.

(Though honesty demands that I say *if*
I'd wanted to take the necessary pains
to scrub the skin's inscription off
I only had an hour between trains.

So the feelings that I had as I stood gazing
and the significance I saw could be a sham,
mere excuses for not patiently erasing
the word sprayed on the grave of dad and mam.)

This pen's all I have of magic wand.
I know this world's so torn but want no other
except for dad who'd hoped from 'the beyond'
a better life than this one, *with* my mother.

Though I don't believe in afterlife at all
and know it's cheating it's hard *not* to make
a sort of furtive prayer from this skin's scrawl,
his UNITED mean 'in Heaven' for their sake,

an accident of meaning to redeem
an act intended as mere desecration
and make the thoughtless spraying of his team
apply to higher things, and to the nation.

Some, where kids use aerosols, use giant signs
to let the people know who's forged their fetters
like PRI CE O WALES above West Yorkshire mines
(no prizes for who nicked the missing letters!).

The big blue star for booze, tobacco ads,
the magnet's monogram, the royal crest,
insignia in neon dwarf the lads
who spray a few odd FUCKS when they're depressed.

Letters of transparent tubes and gas
in Düsseldorf are blue and flash out KRUPP.
Arms are hoisted for the British ruling class
and clandestine, genteel aggro keeps them up.

And there's HARRISON on some Leeds building sites
I've taken in fun as blazoning my name,
which I've also seen on books, in Broadway lights,
so why can't skins with spraycans do the same?

But why inscribe these *graves* with CUNT and SHIT?
Why choose neglected tombstones to disfigure?
This pitman's of last century daubed PAKI GIT,
this grocer Broadbent's aerosolled with NIGGER?

They're there to shock the living, not arouse
the dead from their deep peace to lend support
for the causes skinhead spraycans could espouse.
The dead would want their desecrators caught!

Jobless though they are how can these kids,
even though their team's lost one more game,
believe that the 'Pakis', 'Niggers', even 'Yids'
sprayed on the tombstones here should bear the blame?

What is it that these crude words are revealing?
What is it that this aggro act implies?
Giving the dead their xenophobic feeling
or just a *cri-de-coeur* because man dies?

So what's a cri-de-coeur, *cunt? Can't you speak
the language that yer mam spoke. Think of 'er!
Can yer only get yer tongue round fucking Greek?
Go and fuck yerself with* cri-de-coeur!

'She didn't talk like you do for a start!'
I shouted, turning where I thought the voice had been.
*She didn't understand yer fucking 'art'!
She thought yer fucking poetry obscene!*

I wish on this skin's word deep aspirations,
first the prayer for my parents I can't make,
then a call to Britain and to all the nations
made in the name of love for peace's sake.

*Aspirations, cunt! Folk on t'fucking dole
'ave got about as much scope to aspire
above the shit they're dumped in, cunt, as coal
aspires to be chucked on t'fucking fire.*

'OK, forget the aspirations. Look, I know
United's losing gets you fans incensed
and how far the HARP inside you makes you go
but *all* these Vs: against! against! against!'

Ah'll tell yer then what really riles a bloke.
It's reading on their graves the jobs they did –
butcher, publican and baker. Me, I'll croak
doing t'same nowt ah do now as a kid.

'ard birth ah wor, mi mam says, almost killed 'er.
Death after life on t'dole won't seem as 'ard!
Look at this cunt, Wordsworth, organ builder,
this fucking 'aberdasher Appleyard!

If mi mam's up there, don't want to meet 'er
listening to me list mi dirty deeds,
and 'ave to pipe up to St fucking Peter
ah've been on t'dole all mi life in fucking Leeds!

Then t'Alleluias stick in t'angels' gobs.
When dole-wallahs fuck off to the void
what'll t'mason carve up for their jobs?
The cunts who lieth 'ere wor unemployed?

This lot worked at one job all life through.
Byron, 'Tanner', 'Lieth 'ere interred'.
They'll chisel fucking poet when they do you
and that, yer cunt, 's a crude four-letter word.

'Listen, cunt!' *I* said, 'before you start your jeering
the reason why I want this in a book
's to give ungrateful cunts like you a hearing!'
A book, yer stupid cunt, 's not worth a fuck!

'The only reason why I write this poem at all
on yobs like you who do the dirt on death
's to give some higher meaning to your scrawl.'
Don't fucking bother, cunt! Don't waste your breath!

'You piss-artist skinhead cunt, you wouldn't know
and it doesn't fucking matter if you do,
the skin and poet united fucking Rimbaud
but the *autre* that *je est* is fucking you.'

Ah've told yer, no more Greek . . . That's yer last warning!
Ah'll boot yer fucking balls to Kingdom Come.
They'll find yer cold on t'grave tomorrer morning.
So don't speak Greek. Don't treat me like I'm dumb.

'I've done my bits of mindless aggro too
not half a mile from where we're standing now.'
Yeah, ah bet yer wrote a poem, yer wanker you!
'No, shut yer gob a while. Ah'll tell yer 'ow . . .'

'Herman Darewski's band played operetta
with a wobbly soprano warbling. Just why
I made my mind up that I'd got to get her
with the fire hose I can't say, but I'll try.

It wasn't just the singing angered me.
At the same time half a crowd was jeering
as the smooth Hugh Gaitskell, our MP,
made promises the other half were cheering.

What I hated in those high soprano ranges
was uplift beyond all reason and control
and in a world where you say nothing changes
it seemed a sort of prick-tease of the soul.

I tell you when I heard high notes that rose
above Hugh Gaitskell's cool electioneering
straight from the warbling throat right up my nose
I had all your aggro in *my* jeering.

And I hit the fire extinguisher ON knob
and covered orchestra and audience with spray.
I could run as fast you then. A good job!
They yelled 'damned vandal' after me that day . . .'

And then yer saw the light and gave up 'eavy!
And knew a man's not how much he can sup . . .
Yer reward for growing up's this super-bevvy,
a meths and champagne punch in t'FA Cup.

Ah've 'eard all that from old farts past their prime.
'ow now yer live wi' all yer once detested . . .
Old farts with not much left 'll give me time.
Fuckers like that get folk like me arrested.

Covet not thy neighbour's wife, thy neighbour's riches.
Vicar and cop who say, to save our souls,
Get thee beHind me, Satan, drop their breeches
and get the Devil's dick right up their 'oles!

It was more a *working* marriage that I'd meant,
a blend of masculine and feminine.
Ignoring me, he started looking, bent
on some more aerosolling, for his tin.

'It was more a *working* marriage that I mean!'
Fuck, and save mi soul, eh? That suits me.
Then as if I'd egged him on to be obscene
he added a middle slit to one daubed V.

Don't talk to me of fucking representing
the class yer were born into any more.
Yer going to get 'urt and start resenting
it's not poetry we need in this class war.

Yer've given yerself toffee, cunt. Who needs
yer fucking poufy words. Ah write mi own.
Ah've got mi work on show all ovver Leeds
like this UNITED *'ere on some sod's stone.*

'OK!' (thinking I had him trapped) 'OK!'
'If you're so proud of it, then sign your name
when next you're full of HARP and armed with spray,
next time you take this short cut from the game.'

He took the can, contemptuous, unhurried
and cleared the nozzle and prepared to sign
the UNITED sprayed where mam and dad were buried.
He aerosolled his name. And it was mine.

The boy footballers bawl *Here Comes the Bride*
and drifting blossoms fall onto my head.
One half of me's alive but one half died
when the skin half sprayed my name among the dead.

Half versus half, the enemies within
the heart that can't be whole till they unite.
As I stoop to grab the crushed HARP lager tin
the day's already dusk, half dark, half light.

That UNITED that I'd wished onto the nation
or as reunion for dead parents soon recedes.
The word's once more a mindless desecration
by some HARPoholic yob supporting Leeds.

Almost the time for ghosts I'd better scram.
Though not given much to fears of spooky scaring
I don't fancy an encounter with mi mam
playing Hamlet with me for this swearing.

Though I've a train to catch my step is slow.
I walk on the grass and graves with wary tread
over these subsidences, these shifts below
the life of Leeds supported by the dead.

Further underneath's that cavernous hollow
that makes the gravestones lean towards the town.
A matter of mere time and it will swallow
this place of rest and all the resters down.

I tell myself I've got, say, 30 years.
At 75 this place will suit me fine.
I've never feared the grave but what I fear's
that great worked-out black hollow under mine.

Not train departure time, and not Town Hall
with the great white clock face I can see,
coal, that began, with no man here at all,
as 300 million-year-old plant debris.

5 kids still play at making blossoms fall
and humming as they do *Here Comes the Bride*.
They never seem to tire of their ball
though I hear a woman's voice call one inside.

2 larking boys play bawdy bride and groom.
3 boys in Leeds strip la-la *Lohengrin*.
I hear them as I go through growing gloom
still years away from being skald or skin.

The ground's carpeted with petals as I throw
the aerosol, the HARP can, the cleared weeds
on top of dad's dead daffodils, then go,
with not one glance behind, away from Leeds.

The bus to the station's still the No. 1
but goes by routes that I don't recognise.
I look out for known landmarks as the sun
reddens the swabs of cloud in darkening skies.

Home, home, home, to my woman as the red
darkens from a fresh blood to a dried.
Home, home to my woman, home to bed
where opposites seem sometimes unified.

A pensioner in turban taps his stick
along the pavement past the corner shop,
that sells samosas now, not beer on tick,
to the Kashmir Muslim Club that was the Co-op.

House after house FOR SALE where we'd played cricket
with white roses cut from flour-sacks on our caps,
with stumps chalked on the coal-grate for our wicket,
and every one bought now by 'coloured chaps',

dad's most liberal label as he felt
squeezed by the unfamiliar, and fear
of foreign food and faces, when he smelt
curry in the shop where he'd bought beer.

And growing frailer, 'wobbly on his pins',
the shops he felt familiar with withdrew
which meant much longer tiring treks for tins
that had a label on them that he knew.

And as the shops that stocked his favourites receded
whereas he'd fancied beans and popped next door,
he found that four long treks a week were needed
till he wondered what he bothered eating for.

The supermarket made him feel embarrassed.
Where people bought whole lambs for family freezers
he bought baked beans from check-out girls too harassed
to smile or swap a joke with sad old geezers.

But when he bought his cigs he'd have a chat,
his week's one conversation, truth to tell,
but time also came and put a stop to that
when old Wattsy got bought out by M. Patel.

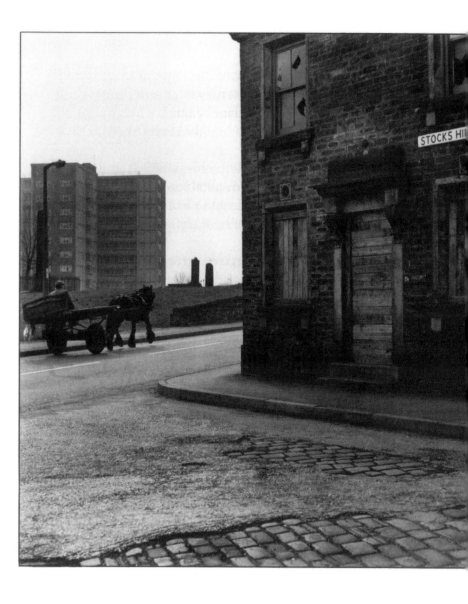

And there, 'Time like an ever rolling stream' 's
what I once trilled behind that boarded front.
A 1000 ages made coal-bearing seams
and even more the hand that sprayed this CUNT

on both Methodist and C of E billboards
once divided in their fight for local souls.
Whichever house more truly was the Lord's
both's pews are filled with cut-price toilet rolls.

Home, home to my woman, never to return
till sexton or survivor has to cram
the bits of clinker scooped out of my urn
down through the rose-roots to my dad and mam.

Home, home to my woman, where the fire's lit
these still chilly mid-May evenings, home to you,
and perished vegetation from the pit
escaping insubstantial up the flue.

Listening to *Lulu,* in our hearth we burn,
as we hear the high Cs rise in stereo,
what was lush swamp club-moss and tree-fern
at least 300 million years ago.

Shilbottle cobbles, Alban Berg high D
lifted from a source that bears your name,
the one we hear decay, the one we see,
the fern from the foetid forest, as brief flame.

This world, with far too many people in,
starts on the TV logo as a taw,
then ping-pong, tennis, football; then one spin
to show us all, then shots of the Gulf War.

As the coal with reddish dust cools in the grate
on the late-night national news we see
police v. pickets at a coke-plant gate,
old violence and old disunity.

The map that's colour-coded Ulster/Eire's
flashed on again as almost every night.
Behind a tiny coffin with two bearers
men in masks with arms show off their might.

The day's last images recede to first a glow
and then a ball that shrinks back to blank screen.
Turning to love, and sleep's oblivion, I know
what the UNITED that the skin sprayed *has* to mean.

Hanging my clothes up, from my parka hood
may and apple petals, browned and creased,
fall onto the carpet and bring back the flood
of feelings their first falling had released.

I hear like ghosts from all Leeds matches humming
with one concerted voice the bride, the bride
I feel united to, *my* bride is coming
into the bedroom, naked, to my side.

The ones we choose to love become our anchor
when the hawser of the blood-tie's hacked, or frays.
But a voice that scorns chorales is yelling: *Wanker!*
It's the aerosolling skin I met today's.

My *alter ego* wouldn't want to know it,
his aerosol vocab would baulk at LOVE,
the skin's UNITED underwrites the poet,
the measures carved below the ones above.

I doubt if 30 years of bleak Leeds weather
and 30 falls of apple and of may
will erode the UNITED binding us together.
And now it's your decision: does it stay?

Next millennium you'll have to search quite hard
to find out where I'm buried but I'm near
the grave of haberdasher Appleyard,
the pile of HARPs, or some new neonned beer.

Find Byron, Wordsworth, or turn left between
one grave marked Broadbent, one marked Richardson.
Bring some solution with you that can clean
whatever new crude words have been sprayed on.

If love of art, or love, gives you affront
that the grave I'm in's graffitied then, maybe,
erase the more offensive FUCK and CUNT
but leave, with the worn UNITED, one small v.

Victory? For vast, slow, coal-creating forces
that hew the body's seams to get the soul.
Will Earth run out of her 'diurnal courses'
before repeating her creation of black coal?

But choose a day like I chose in mid-May
or earlier when apple and hawthorn tree,
no matter if boys boot their ball all day,
cling to their blossoms and won't shake them free.

If, having come this far, somebody reads
these verses, and he/she wants to understand,
face this grave on Beeston Hill, your back to Leeds,
and read the chiselled epitaph I've planned:

Beneath your feet's a poet, then a pit.
Poetry supporter, if you're here to find
how poems can grow from (beat you to it!) SHIT
find the beef, the beer, the bread, then look behind.

'The riff-raff takes over'

by NEIL ASTLEY,
editor, Bloodaxe Books

Thomas Gray composed his Elegy in a quiet country churchyard. Two centuries later, Tony Harrison wrote *v.* in a vandalised cemetery in Leeds during the Miners' Strike. It begins with words by Arthur Scargill and ends – like Gray's Elegy – with the poet's own epitaph. It embodies those two extremes in its language and concerns, from Gray's poem on the one hand, which is much more than just a neat literary model, to Scargill's tribute to his father, who believed that people's destinies are shaped by their own mastery of words.

Harrison's concern, like Gray's, is less with mortality than with frustrated human potential. Gray's 'mute inglorious Miltons' have their counterparts in the local artisans Byron and Wordsworth laid to rest near Harrison's parents in Beeston cemetery. The nihilistic skinhead is what Harrison might have been, but for his education; and both protagonists, both Harrisons, define themselves and their alienation through their use of language.

The skinhead is contemptuous of words he wouldn't use at home: words from another culture, another Britain, the language of privilege and authority, used by those who've put him down. Harrison spits back his repetitive four-letter expletives, using the youth's own words not only to show how his thinking has been inhibited by his poverty of language, but also to voice the frustrations of his class (something which the skinhead says he doesn't need from him).

The conflict in Harrison's poetry is far more complex than a simple 'them' *versus* 'us' confrontation, for he has himself become estranged from his working-class background in acquiring the language he now uses subversively on behalf of the dispossessed and inarticulate. At the same time, his subject-matter, class, has become something of an embarrassment, for many people in Britain now believe (or pretend) that class no longer matters, just as they think there is no excuse for not finding a job or for getting swallowed up in the poverty trap. However, Harrison's isolation makes his voice all the more necessary at a time when market forces are supposed to dictate our responses to social and individual needs. As Douglas Dunn wrote in a review of *v.*, Harrison is 'squarely on the side of Old Left decencies'.

When Bloodaxe first published *v.* in 1985, we couldn't claim that a few thousand copies of a poetry book could do much to challenge those kinds of complacent assumptions, even if it was – as *Tribune* said – 'the most outstanding social poem of the past 25 years'. Richard Eyre's Channel Four film of *v.* changed all that. Thanks to the publicity, generated initially by the tabloid press, the poem reached an audience of several million – and not just those who saw the programme but also the readership of *The Independent*, which printed the whole poem.

The political and cultural issues debated in the press are still current and of fundamental importance. In *The Journal* (Newcastle), David Isaacs linked the attacks on the film to 'politically motivated hysteria' and to recent government cutbacks in arts funding, political appointments at the BBC and threats of institutionalised censorship'. In other papers, columnists objected to the poem's 'offensive' language but seemed more discomforted by the effrontery of its frank representation of a side of life they didn't want to know about.

It is difficult to read the poem now without becoming engaged also with the wider issues raised both by the film itself and by the controversy it stimulated. Because of this, we asked Tony Harrison to allow us to expand *v.* into a larger book and include press articles and other matter relating to the film. In agreeing to this, he left the choice of what to include to me. What follows is not a complete compilation but is presented as a representative selection of press and public comment both for and against the poem and the film. I have tried where possible to use articles in full, and I must thank the newspapers, writers, Channel Four and others for their kind permission to reproduce their material in the book.

The only piece written specially for this edition was Richard Eyre's article, although its partisan point of view is more than balanced by the negative voices of other writers represented in the compilation. Of those I feel I must make special mention of the former Conservative MP Sir Gilbert Longden, writer of the letter to *The Independent* on page 68, who wrote: 'You may certainly use my letter in the Independent of 2 November 1987. I would only add, in the words of John Simon (the American Art critic, not the English statesman) which embrace all "art" forms: "once you admit Jackson Pollock to the ranks of great painters, anybody can paint; once junk can be sculpture, anybody can be a sculptor ... the riff-raff takes over."'

Such men are dangerous

by RICHARD EYRE,
director of the film of v.

In Russia they used to kill their poets *pour encourager les autres.*
The reward for the English poet is at best indifference and at
worst becoming Poet Laureate. With *v.*, Tony Harrison violated
both ends of that spectrum. Whatever was invoked by the poem,
it was not indifference. Indignation, outrage, joy, sorrow, pity
perhaps and paradoxically, for a man who would violently shun
any form of honour, he became the uncrowned poet laureate – a
truly public poet.

I first became aware of the rumbling storm provoked by
Channel 4's intention to show the film of *v.* when I was making
another film which also provoked severe climatic disturbances,
Tumbledown. There were similarities in the response to both
films. In both cases, before the transmission, in fact before anyone
even on the production team had seen the finished films, there
was a chorus of outrage, misrepresentation, prejudice, insult,
bullying and condescension from MPs, journalists, peers and
pundits. Popular newspapers, as ever, found rich resources of
moral indignation. I was standing in a North London car park on
a grey dawn, waiting for the day's filming to begin when a cheery
make-up assistant thrust a copy of the *Daily Mail* into my hand.
'You've made the front page,' she said. I read, and I hope I do full
value to the pungent prose, 'FOUR-LETTER TV POEM FURY!'
Only with hindsight was I grateful to the *Mail* and their even more
downmarket clones for having unwittingly brought to the poem
an audience whose size could never have been imagined without
their gift of free publicity. It was an audience, I think, who largely
came to the poem out of curiosity and was surprised to find that
not only could they understand it, but that they were moved,
amused, even educated by it.

The film's editor was a man who, like many victims of our
educational system, had been turned off poetry at an early age. 'It
was,' he said, 'not for me.' One of the greatest pleasures of
making the film was watching Ray become drawn into the poem
so that he felt each nuance, each rhyme, each rhythm, each shift of
thought with an ever increasing vividness. Indeed, all of us
involved in making the film became evangelistic in support of the

poem: its miraculous appeal to the head and the heart, its way of yoking sophisticated and ambitious philosophical speculation to minute physical observations; its astonishing variety contained within an unvarying scheme of rhyme and scansion; its pessimism as much as its optimism and above all, its endless celebration of the ambiguities of what it wouldn't be too grand to call the human condition. We all thought, as Ray put it, that the poem was fucking amazing. I still do, and when Tony told me that a parents action group had succeeded in persuading the Manchester Education Committee (via the office of that renowned figure of the new enlightenment, James Anderton) to withdraw his poetry from the school curriculum, I felt once again that as in Russia, poetry was dangerous. The Russian poet Gumilyov (who was shot) said that dead words smell badly. These are the words of the acknowledged legislators of our world who proscribe, censor, inhibit and monitor what we should read and see and by implication, think and feel.

If I had the slightest influence over educational policy in this country, I'd see that *v.* was a set text in every school in the country, but of course if we lived in that sort of country, the poem wouldn't have needed to be written.

RICHARD EYRE
National Theatre, April 1989

Clear road for rude ode

RICHARD BROOKS
Media Editor

A CONTROVERSIAL poem, containing the most sexually explicit language ever heard on British television, has been given the go-ahead by the Independent Broadcasting Authority.

However, Channel 4, which had planned to broadcast the filmed version of 'v', a poem written and read by Tony Harrison and directed by Richard Eyre, director-designate of the National Theatre, in mid-evening, has now re-scheduled it for 11.30 p.m. 'It was a mistake to have thought it could have gone out earlier,' said C4.

The filmed poem went to the IBA's full board and was cleared after a heated debate.

It is very unusual for the authority to view any programme in advance for clearance. While mindful of current sensitivity over TV sex and violence the IBA concluded that the poem's 'artistic integrity' was the determining factor. It would have been impossible to ' bleep ' or cut the poem.

Channel 4 will now show ' v.' (it stands for versus, although it is a pun on verses), at 11.30 p.m. on 4 November, rather than its scheduled mid-evening slot on 29 October to follow the Booker Prize ceremony.

The 45-minute filmed version of Harrison's poem is set in a Leeds graveyard. It is interspersed with footage of war and inner-city dereliction.

■ Radio 4's ' Radio Active ' programme—itself a parody of a radio station—has again landed the BBC in trouble. Thousands found its recent edition on religious broadcasting blasphemous, and the repeat was heavily censored.

SUNDAY 11 OCTOBER 1987
THE OBSERVER

FOUR-LET TV POEM

By JOHN DEANS and GARRY JENKINS

BROADCASTERS are lining up for a head-on clash with the political establishment over a planned Channel 4 programme featuring a torrent of four-letter filth.

Outraged MPs last night demanded an immediate ban on the screening, which will unleash the most explicitly sexual language yet beamed into the nation's living rooms.

And the pressure will be on Home Secretary Douglas Hurd, who is proposing to set up a new watchdog Broadcasting Standards Council, to crack down on the media bosses now.

The cascade of expletives will pour out to viewers at the rate of two a minute during the 45-minute show on November 4. The crudest, most offensive word is used 17 times.

MONDAY 12 OCTOBER 1987
DAILY MAIL

TER FURY

'It's some MP reciting a poem'

The programme, a filmed recital of a poem called 'v' written and read by Newcastle poet Tony Harrison, was given the all-clear by the Independent Broadcasting Authority after it took the unusual step of showing it to the full board.

Originally it was to have been screened in a mid-evening slot but Channel 4 has now put it back to 11.30 p.m.

'V' written by Harrison in 1985, is based on obscene graveyard graffiti and uses football hooligan slang. The title stands for 'versus' and when published in an anthology of the poet's work it was dedicated to miners' leader Arthur Scargill.

Last night Tory MP Gerald Howarth called for the programme to be withdrawn.

'This is another clear case of the broadcasters trying to assault the public by pushing against the barriers of what is acceptable, on the basis that the more effing and blinding they can get into everyday programmes, the better.'

Mr Howarth, who last year won a major legal battle with the BBC over claims that Fascists had infiltrated the Tory Party, described 50-year-old Harrison as 'another probable Bolshie poet seeking to impose his frustrations on the rest of us'

Another Tory MP, Teddy Taylor, also appealed to Channel 4 chiefs to see sense.

'Obviously Channel 4 is the place for experiment, and for a bit of variety, but a poem stuffed full of obscenities is clearly so objectionable that it will lead to the Government being forced to take, action it would prefer not to have to take," he added.

And clean-up campaigner Mary Whitehouse said: "The sooner the Government brings broadcasting under the obscenity laws, the better for everyone and particularly the public.

But 'v' was defended by the poet, the IBA and Channel 4.

Harrison said: 'The language is an integral part of the poem. It is the language of the football hooligan and is seen and heard every day.'

'I don't see that it should merit any fuss whatsoever.

The IBA said the film had been viewed by the board at the request of Director-General John Whitney.

A spokesman said: 'It was considered very carefully, especially given out statutory duty as fas as matters of taste and decency are concerned. But we came to the view that it was acceptable.'

A Channel 4 spokesman said: 'We stand by our decision, which was taken after careful consideration and full discussion with the IBA.'

But he accepted that the film 'may be disturbing to some', and a warning will be given to viewers before it is shown.

Battle to ban shock TV poem

A SHOCKING TV poem—packed with obscene four-letter words—is to be broadcast despite protests by clean-up campaigners.

Channel 4 are to go ahead with a filmed recital of "V" by Newcastle poet Tony Harrison which contains 90 swear words.

Claim

It will contain some of the most explicit language ever broadcast.

Mary Whitehouse and several MPs have asked TV chiefs to reconsider the screening at 11.30pm on November 4.

But a Channel 4 spokesman said: "We stand by our decision."

MONDAY 12 OCTOBER 1987

THE SUN

MONDAY 12 OCTOBER 1987

DAILY EXPRESS

Scargill: Dedication

Scargill poem is the pits

TV BOSSES last night defended their decision to broadcast a poem containing a string of four-letter words as a tribute to Arthur Scargill.

The torrent of foul language will be seen in a Channel 4 programme by respected Newcastle poet Tony Harison.

He will recite his controversial work "V" which is dedicated to the miners' leader in a late night show on November 4.

Clean

But Channel 4 chiefs who took the decision after "careful consideration believe the 11.30 time slot makes it acceptable.

However TV clean-up campaigner Mary Whitehouse has called for the show to be cancelled.

The decision to screen the work comes in the wake of Home Secretary Douglas Hurd's decision to set up a broadcasting standards council to clean up TV.

Demand for ban on four-letter poem defied by Channel 4

By Harvey Lee, Television Correspondent

CHANNEL 4 yesterday stood by its decision to broadcast a poetry recital containing a stream of four-letter words in a late-night slot.

The programme, to be shown on Nov 4 during the channel's fifth anniversary week, has caused a political storm.

MPs and clean-up campaigner Mrs Mary Whitehouse have called for it to be banned. They are outraged by the explicit language used in the filmed recital of "v", by Tony Harrison, the Newcastle poet, dramatist and television presenter.

Channel 4 described the poem, first published in 1985, as a lament for lost values. The title stands for "versus", a pun on "verses", and represents divisions in British society.

Rare step

The programme, made by London Weekend Television, has already been moved from a mid-evening slot to 11pm.

The full board of Channel 4 vetted the film before deciding to screen it, and in a rare step Mr John Whitney, director-general of the Independent Broadcasting Authority, also asked his board members to view it.

Mr Harrison recites the poem during the 40-minute programme, filmed before an audience and in a Leeds graveyard, in which the cameras show his family vault desecrated by obscene graffiti.

The programme was directed by Mr Richard Eyre, director-designate of the National Theatre, which has staged several Greek plays adapted by the poet. Mr Harrison also made "Loving Memory," a BBC-2 series on burial customs.

A Channel 4 spokesman said: "Channel 4 stands by its decision, taken after careful consideration and full discussion with the IBA, to show the programme in a late slot. The programme may be disturbing to some, but will be appropriately signposted."

Mr Gerald Haworth, Tory MP for Cannock and Burntwood and a campaigner for tighter controls on television, is to ask the IBA to withdraw the programme.

He said: "I find it astonishing when the media are right in the public eye, that the IBA is prepared to authorise a programme, admittedly going out after 9pm, which seems to contravene the Broadcasting Act.

"This states that they must not broadcast anything which offends against good taste and public feeling. To string a load of expletives together seems to be in clear breach of the law."

Mr Teddy Taylor, Tory MP for Southend East, said: "If Channel 4 had any sense, it would not transmit this cascade of obscenities. Quite apart from causing great offence, this is asking for trouble at a time when the Government is looking carefully and urgently at violence and obscenity on TV."

Offensive words

The row has blown up only days after Mr Hurd, Home Secretary, announced plans to set up a Broadcasting Standards Council. The Government also intends to remove broadcasting's exemption from the Obscene Publications Act.

Mr Harrison said: "The offensive words have been taken out of context by people who have neither seen the programme nor read my poem. It does seem an artificially created storm.

"I have read the poem in public many times in the past two years, without any objections being raised. Audiences seem rather moved by it.

"If we want to debate some of the obscenities in our culture, including the way graveyards have been outrageously graffitied by four-letter words and swastikas, we must represent them.

"Language of that nature ought not to have been daubed over a grave where my parents are buried. I was appalled and I wanted to write about it."

TUESDAY 13 OCTOBER 1987

DAILY TELEGRAPH

43

FROM BAD TO VERSE...

Fury over TV poem

A PLAN to televise a poem packed with obscenities caused outrage last night.

ITV chiefs intend to screen a reading of Tony Harrison's verse "V" which is full of four-letter words.

Furious Tory MP Gerald Owart has demanded that the Channel 4 programme be banned.

Shocker . . . we have censored some of the poem for family reading

"It is full of expletives and can't see that it serves any artistic purpose whatsoever," he said yesterday.

Shocked

But the IBA, the ITV's ruling body, said last night they have no intention of refusing permission for the show to be screened next month.

The poem is based on Harrison's experience of finding his family's gravestone covered in crude graffiti.

The Tyneside poet said yesterday: "I think people are condemning this poem out of hand without having even heard it or read it.

"I have read the poem to scores of different audiences over the last couple of years.

TUESDAY 13 OCTOBER 1987
THE STAR

45

Ignorant assault

NEWCASTLE-based poet Tony Harrison found himself at the centre of unwanted controversy yesterday when it was revealed that his epic poem, v, has been made into a television programme for Channel 4. DAVID ISAACS offers a personal view of the row.

IF ANYONE was left with a lingering doubt that the Arts are today under siege by an increasingly Right-wing Establishment, those doubts will have been removed by yesterday's ignorant assault on Tony Harrison, the quiet and likeable Yorkshireman who has spent the last 20 years living in Gosforth.

We have already seen cutbacks in Arts Council funding, the carefully-considered appointments to positions of power within the BBC, the threats of institutionalised censorship. But yesterday's crude attempt to villify a man who has been described as "our greatest modern theatrical poet" represents a new and more dangerous kind of threat.

Much depends on the official reaction, of course. I am willing to give Home Secretary Douglas Hurd the benefit of the doubt by supposing him to possess too intelligent and liberal a mind to be swayed by this kind of politically-motivated hysteria.

But we should not respond with matching hysteria. We should take a long, cool look at the facts. And they are these:

* That Tony Harrison is a major artist who has produced many great works for the National Theatre, including a version of The Oresteia.
* That his translation of Moliere's The Misanthrope was so highly regarded that it was even translated back into French.
* That his acclaimed version of The Mysteries trilogy, staged by the National Theatre in 1985, was subsequently seen on Channel 4.
* That he is in international demand from the world of opera as a librettist.

In any other country, he would be hailed as a national cultural hero. Here, he is insulted by an obscure Conservative MP called Gerald Howarth, who describes him as "another probable Bolshie poet seeking to impose his frustrations on the rest of us."

As someone who read the poem when it was first published two years ago, I can tell you that my second move was to invite my daughter, then aged 17, to read it.

For it concerns her generation. It concerns the inarticulate young who express themselves in violent language at football grounds up and down the country and scrawl obscene grafitti on gravestones in the Leeds cemetery where Harrison's parents are buried.

Yes, v. uses those offensive four-letter words. It uses them liberally. But the poem is a scream of outrage against that whole sub-culture which can find no other way of expressing itself, a cry of rage against the degradation of thought, emotion, imagination and language.

I do not know whether his point is being misunderstood because of a lack of knowledge, sensitivity or intelligence. But I would like to think it could not be put down to an orchestrated and deliberate attempt to misrepresent.

I would like to think that.

47

To show V or not to show V

☐ THE ROW over the televising of Tony Harrison's poem V will be the dinner-party topic of the next few weeks. "A cascade of obscenity," says Teddy Taylor MP; "a probable Bolshy" — George Howarth.

V is a 448-line meditation on the desecration by graffiti of Beeston Cemetery in Leeds, where Harrison's parents are buried. It has a lot of dirty words in it, or rather, it has the three or four dirty words everyone knows, repeated many times.

It is difficult to quote, not because of the obscenity, but the prolixity. Harrison notes, for instance, the word "United" sprayed on his parents' tomb, which is a poignant little image. But he then insists on explaining, over several stanzas, that it is poignant because although it *actually* refers to Leeds United FC, it *could also* be taken to refer to his parents' union in heaven, *or even* to the disunited nature of modern society.

Harrison is the kind of pedant who will never let an image unfold in the reader's mind, will never make a point once if he can make it three times, and like a pub bore will never let you go until he is *quite sure* you have got the joke. Philip Larkin's poem, Sunny Prestatyn, uses the same image of graffiti as its theme, makes essentially the same point about the desecration of an innocent past, and even uses a few dirty words — but does it with grace, wit and in 24 lines.

Tony Harrison is one of the few poets in the country who actually make money, which has always baffled me. From The Loiners (1970) to The Fire Gap (1985) his poetry has been humourlessly didactic, crammed with "relevance" and shackled to relentless rhymes and rumty-tum rhythms, like a kind of politicised Pam Ayres.

Not that this in an argument for banning V. I have never believed there is much point in banning anything, apart from "Celebrity Squares". The banning of Denis Potter's "Brimstone and Treacle" only gave it an underground reputation it did not deserve. The Lady Chatterley trial turned one of D H Lawrence's most mediocre novels into his most celebrated. If V is banned it will distort literary judgment for a decade. The best way of consigning it to deserved oblivion is to put it out at 11.30 p m on Channel 4 — which, of course, is exactly what is proposed.

FRIDAY 16 OCTOBER 1987

DAILY TELEGRAPH

Hugh Hebert defends TV's version of Tony Harrison's controversial poem V

Vindications of mortality

WHO said "My father still reads the dictionary every day. He says your life depends on your power to master words." You guessed. Arthur Scargill, in 1982. This odd snippet is the epigraph for Tony Harrison's long poem V, which this week caused much heartburn among the kind of MP who sits up counting how many four-letter words appear in a programme scheduled to go out half an hour before midnight.

It's easy to laugh off the rent-a-howl raised by the right-wing press on these occasions. V in itself is not an issue, four days after it was raised — Channel 4 and the IBA are standing firm on the decision to go ahead on November 4. But this is exactly the kind of programme that might fall foul of the proposals to bring broadcasting under the obscenity laws.

V has been in printed form since it came out in London Review of Books 2½ years ago. Richard Eyre's film is mostly a complete reading of the poem by Harrison to a pub room audience. So if under the rumoured legislation, the television version of V were prosecuted for obscenity, would that involve also seizing all the copies of the published version? And if not, why not? Would it involve charging Harrison with an obscene act for reading it in public?

The absurdities are so obvious that they have to be underlined. But there are two points about taking up cudgels in this version of the poem. The first is that it is a better television film about V than the poem is a poem. The second is that the words that the Daily Mail has called "A torrent of filth" really are intrinsic to the poem. It could not exist without them.

At one level, this is a long, meditative, sometimes quite moving piece about the poet's relationship to his dead parents, about the way his work with words relates to his father's work as a baker.

It is set in a cemetery high above Harrison's native Leeds. Many of the graves have been sprayed with grafitti with the usual run of expletives, or sometimes with the word "United", which appears on his own parents' memorial, and stands of course for Leeds United; it is not a statement of some mystical faith. It is a poem about the use of language, the anger of being inarticulate.

To understand Harrison's intense feeling about that, you need to know that his father, an obsessive figure in his poetry, was not an articulate man; and that one of Harrison's uncles was a stammerer, and another was actually dumb. The poem is partly an expression of his own guilt at living off a facility of expression that was wholly denied to his male forebears; and his guilt at having work when those other inarticulates, the grafitti lads, have none except plying their spray cans.

V contains all the usual four-letter words known to most children by the time they are, what, 10? Younger? They are quoted here as grafitti, and in one section where Harrison is arguing with a skinhead alter ego, " fuck " does appear many times. I'm not sure whether the repetition makes it more offensive to those offended by it once, but it certainly emasculates the word itself. That is the paradox of the repetition.

The poem is not about sex. Eyre's film is explicit in the best sense, it enables us to see Harrison's poem in its proper setting. We see him in the Leeds graveyard, see the grafitti on the tombs, because this is a short cut from the Leeds United ground back into town.

HARRISON : Poet of industrial decline

We see — maybe a bit too literally — Harrison's puns on the title V spelt out. V for Victory, and Versus, and Verses. And we see and hear Harrison reading the poem to a rapt audience, which is more important than the rest, because even the most private of Harrison's poems work far better in performance than on the page.

It's a good but not a great poem — for me it is too sentimental and masochistic, its genuine feeling is too intellectualised. But it's a poem deeply felt and linking some of the dominant themes of contemporary British writing : industrial decline (the stones lean this way and that, because of mining subsidence), post-industrial despair. It even has a few jokes. Though none quite as absurd as wanting to ban it from being broadcast through the midnight hour.

SATURDAY 17 OCTOBER 1987

THE GUARDIAN

AUBERON WAUGH'S COLUMN

FEW PEOPLE IN this country can be more persecuted by modern "poets" than I am in my capacity as editor of the *Literary Review.*

They continue to send in their rubbish by every post. Some — not much of it — is obscene, but I decided it might be a good idea to send on all the obscene material to Channel 4 when I learned from Teddy Taylor and other concerned folk that it was planning to broadcast "a cascade of obscenities" from the lips of Tony Harrison, the Newcastle poet, on November 4.

But that was before I read Harrison's poem, rather tiresomely called *V* and deliberately written in the form of Gray's *Elegy Written in a Country Churchyard.* It describes how he visits his parents' grave in a Leeds cemetery, now littered with beer cans, and vandalised by obscene graffiti. Much of the poem is an imaginary dialogue with the skinhead responsible for scrawling the obscenities.

It is not without its faults, being too long and repetitive. The argument wanders a little, and some of the stanzas work better than others. But I found it well written and extremely moving. People are making fools of themselves who object to the rude words, since they are essential to the scene he is describing and the dialogue which ensues. I urge everybody who is remotely interested in what is happening to the North of England to listen to it on November 4.

SUNDAY 18 OCTOBER 1987
SUNDAY TELEGRAPH

Gerald Howarth MP	Peter Levi	Harold Pinter	Melvin Bragg
'obscenities'	'deserves study'	'broadcast it'	'relevant'

Literati back TV poem attacked by MPs as 'filth'

by Geordie Greig

BRITAIN'S literary establishment has joined ranks to support a controversial four-letter word poem which Tory MPs are campaigning to get banned from a Channel 4 programme next month.

Leading poets, academics and writers say the poem, V, which was last week described by Tory MPs as "a torrent of obscene language" and a "stream of four-letter filth", should be televised.

The literary supporters say that Tony Harrison, an acclaimed modern poet, has been the subject of a hypocritical and unfair attack.

The poem is an impassioned account by Harrison, a National Theatre playwright, on finding graffiti sprayed on his parents' gravestone by a Leeds United skinhead.

Channel 4, with the full backing of the Independent Broadcasting Authority, plans to screen a 40-minute film at 11pm on November 4. It shows Harrison reading the poem in different parts of Leeds, his home town including the graveyard.

But Gerald Howarth, Tory MP for Cannock and Burntwood, who put forward the Obscene Publications Bill in April, has condemned the 47 expletives in the 448-line poem. "It contains a cascade of obscenities and it is ridiculous to call it art," he said. He

will seek resignations in the broadcasting world if it goes ahead.

However, the attack on Harrison has rankled many literary figures. Peter Levi, Oxford University's professor of poetry, said: "It plays off vernacular language against formality marvellously. As a work of complex thought and feeling it deserves to be studied." Levi does not believe it is too offensive to be read on air.

Harold Pinter, the playwright, is in favour of V appearing: "The criticism against the poem has been offensive, juvenile and, of course, philistine. It should certainly be broadcast."

In the poem, Harrison relates an imaginary conversation between himself and the scrawling skinhead. The narrative questions the social and political reasons behind such "mindless desecration". Harrison suggests, however, that the skinhead should not shoulder blame alone: "It isn't all his fault though. Much is ours." The poem reaches its peak with the two characters

becoming one and the same persona.

Auberon Waugh, editor of the Literary Review, described V as "an interesting pastiche of Thomas Gray's Elegy in A Country Churchyard, only it is set in Leeds. Anyone with an interest in life in the northeast should watch it."

Melvin Bragg enthused: "He has brilliantly taken classical themes such as death, graves, and growing up and dealt with them in a way relevant to young people today."

V could soon be taught in schools. Brian Tyler, the headmaster of Kingswood school, Corby, Northants, said: "There has been a knee-jerk reaction to the bad language. The poem would make an interesting A-level text. TV quiz shows and advertisements with their values of greed and selfishness are far more dangerous than the bad language in V."

Before leaving for a reading holiday in Turkey, Harrison said last week: "The offensive words have been taken out of context by people who have neither seen the programme nor read my poem. It does seem an artificially-created storm."

SUNDAY 18 OCTOBER 1987
SUNDAY TIMES

Bernard Levin: the way we live now

An adult's garden of verse

Some time in the early 1980s, Mr Tony Harrison, one of the finest and deepest poets now writing in English (he is in addition our leading translator of dramatic verse, with versions of *Le Misanthrope* and the *Oresteia* that have never been bettered and probably never will be), was in the habit of making time to visit his parents' grave whenever (he no longer lived near the cemetery) he had to change trains in the area. On one such visit, he found that the cemetery had been desecrated by skinheads, who had sprayed aerosolled obscenities — though not, as we shall see, only obscenities — on the headstones and monuments, including the grave where his parents lay.

This gave him a shock; it also, however, became the seed of what later flowered into one of the most powerful, profound and haunting long poems of modern times; some 3,500 words in 112 four-line stanzas, rhyming ABAB. The poem is a meticulously controlled yell of rage and hope combined, a poisoned dart aimed with deadly precision at the waste of human potential, shaped by a master poet with a rich and instinctive feel for the language, a penetrating eye that misses nothing it looks on, and an exceptionally ingenious capacity for using innocent word-play to make a telling case. The poem was published in the *London Review of Books*, and later in an anthology of his poetry; his verse in general, and this poem in particular, has received the highest commendation from a very wide range of critics and fellow poets.

The poem is called *v.* Just that; *v.* The v stands for versus; it is the symbol that links football clubs to their opponents of the week, and since the graveyard graffiti were spray-painted by supporters of Leeds United, the theme recurred throughout the area of desecration. Mr Harrison's use of it, however, is far wider; he uses the v as a symbol of division, as he uses the United of the football club as a symbol of harmony. Let him speak in his own words:

These vs are all the versuses of life
from LEEDS v. DERBY, Black/White
and (as I've known to my cost) man v. wife,
Communist v. Fascist, Left v. Right,
class v. class as bitter as before,
the unending violence of US and THEM,
personified in 1984
by Coal Board MacGregor and the NUM,
Hindu/Sikh, soul/body, heart v. mind,
East/West, male/female, and the ground
these fixtures are fought on's man, resigned
to hope from his future what his past
               has never found.

The poem is a threnody; for his dead parents, for the "skins" who have deadened themselves, for all the wasted hopes of the world. It is written in fire, and the fuel is a monolithic integrity; Mr Harrison is not only a poet of consummate gifts, but evidently (I have not had the pleasure of his direct acquaintance) a man of exceptional quality.

So much by way of introduction; now for what this is all about. The befouled cemetery, strewn with empty beer cans, bore also in graffiti form words other than those connected with the skinheads' favourite team. Obscenities (have you ever noticed how few they are?) were repeated incessantly throughout the burial ground — as, indeed, they are repeated on any available bit of wall, derelict building, underpass or other structure wherever two or three skins are gathered together.

Now the words in question, though on the whole they are not used in polite society, or for that matter in society sufficiently literate to express itself more eloquently, are known, with their meanings, to everyone in the country except *very* young children. They are, however, subject to a strict taboo; not the taboo which simply excludes them from most civilized discourse, but a much stranger form, which is based on the conviction that, first, the words are *not* known to anyone other than habitual users of them, and that, second, if they are spoken in ordinary conversation they may provoke no more than distaste, but if they are published, either physically in a newspaper or verbally on television or radio, they will have generally unspecified but very terrible consequences, which will have the effect of undermining all moral standards and restraints, leading in turn to a state of affairs in which the very sheep in their pens and the spaniels in their kennels will not be safe from even the most extreme forms of depravity, while as for the au pair — but a veil must be drawn somewhere.

The taboo has one subsidiary form which is actually odder than the basic theme. If the words are printed with only their initial letters, followed by asterisks or dashes ("F***", say, or "Sh–"), they are at once and entirely robbed of their dreadful power, and may be read by the most sensitive souls without harm or danger. (No one has ever been able to explain this phenomenon; come to think of it, no one has ever been able to explain the main taboo, either.)

We return to Mr Harrison. In his poem, he uses these words very freely, in two distinct modes. The first is, so to speak, quotation; he records the spattering of the words amid the graves. The second is in the form of an imaginary dialogue, conceived as the skins' answer to his implied rebuke, in which they express themselves as best they can — the best being, because of their limited vocabulary, with a profusion of the words in question. As, for instance:

> ❝ Do we not show ourselves as a nation of laughing-stocks when one of our outstanding literary artists proposes to read one of his most telling creations in public and is greeted by screams of outrage? ❞

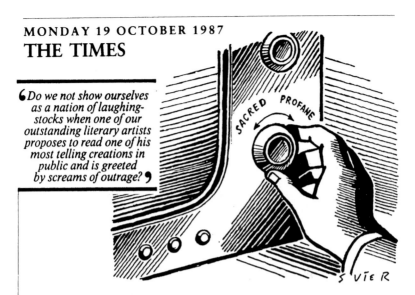

Aspirations, cunt! folk on t'fucking dole
'ave got about as much scope to aspire
above the shit they're dumped in, cunt, as coal
aspires to be chucked on t'fucking fire.
Yer've given yerself toffee, cunt. Who needs
yer fucking poufy words. Ah write mi own.
Ah've got mi work on show all over Leeds
like this UNITED 'ere on some sod's stone.

The scene now shifts to Channel Four, which has announced its intention of broadcasting the whole poem, read by Mr Harrison himself, on November 4 at 11pm. To hear a poet of such talent read a poem of such quality will be a rare and memorable experience; I shall ensure that I see the programme.

So, I hope, will anyone who despairs of modern poetry; so, inevitably, will be many who think (rightly, for all I can say) that they might get a thrill from hearing impolite words on television. But so, alas, will the inglorious company of the smut-hounds, the book-burners, the sniffers-out of words and expressions that awake (as well as their prurience) both their alarm at, and their fascination with, such terms.

Most of them have not waited for the broadcast, nor have they thought it necessary to read the poem before denouncing it. In addition to the usual dial-a-quote MPs and Mrs Whitehouse (oozing self-righteousness as usual), a wholly factitious campaign has sprung up, demanding the cancellation of the programme (which is no more likely to have been seen by the demanders than the denouncers). In particular, the *Daily Mail* covered most of its front page the other day with a headline reading "TV FOUR-LETTER POEM FURY" (in newspaper parlance such words as "fury" and "storm", used in that context, signal to the knowledgeable that the

entire campaign is spurious), and as the terrible hour approaches, we may expect them to intensify their imaginary indignation.

Here I pause, to peach. I have heard the editor of the *Daily Mail*, Sir David English (a very parfit gentil knight, too!) say "Fuck". He did not say it loudly, nor with great emphasis, and I *think* he looked round first to see whether there were any ladies within earshot, but say it he did. (In all fairness, I must add that I have used the word myself, but many years ago Sir David and I both worked at the *Daily Express*, so perhaps I picked it up from him then.)

Oh, asterisk, dash and blank; have we really got to go through all this yet again? Must the ghost of Mervyn Griffith-Jones rise gibbering in its winding-sheet to demand that our wives and servants should be protected from such things? Is Ken Tynan (what a fine, honest and beautifully written biography his widow has just published, incidentally) to be hauled out of Purgatory to testify to the fact that he was the first man to say "Fuck" on television, and that the world did not come to an end because of it, either at once or gradually? Do we not show ourselves as a nation of laughing-stocks when one of our most outstanding literary artists proposes to read one of his most telling creations in public and is greeted by screams of hysterical outrage from people who have almost certainly never heard of him, and have probably not read any poem written later than Wordsworth on the daffodils?

Well, if we must, we must. For my part, I think I have made my position fairly clear, and all I need to add is that I hope Channel Four will stand firm against the Yahoos. And, perhaps, that Mr Harrison's *Selected Poems* is published by Penguin, is in print, costs £4.95, includes *v.*, and demonstrates, far more conclusively than any article of mine, what squalid nonsense the campaign against him is.

53

Ronald Butt

Disdain versus manners

It is a sensible rule of thumb for columnists not to take issue with other columnists' arguments. If I seem to break it now, this is appearance rather than reality. I am taking issue here not with an argument but with an act of social behaviour, which is a much greater breach of convention than for me to discuss another column

On Monday Mr Bernard Levin chose to reproduce a verse of unmitigated obscenity to illustrate an argument. A poet, Mr Tony Harrison, who is well known as poets go these days, and is rightly well regarded for some of his work, including translations for the National Theatre, has written some verses called *v.* (for versus). Having read the whole work I have an opinion about how far it constitutes poetry, but I am not offering literary criticism and will only say that I do not think anyone could construe the two verses reproduced by Mr Levin as poetry, if poetry has anything to do with heightened awareness.

The first was of harmless banality, describing the "versuses" of contemporary life in doggerel of a kind that might be written by a politically minded youth who had well absorbed the sociological platitudes of the age about conflict, including the unending violence of "us" and "them" personified by "Coal Board MacGregor and the NUM." The second was simply concentrated obscenity. The verses were inspired by Mr Harrison's resentment on finding the head-stones of the cemetery where his parents are buried desecrated by the obscenities of skinheads using spray cans.

Mr Harrison was deeply outraged and offended. Who would not be? So he wrote his poem (let us call it that), in which he reproduced the filthy and aggressive abuse of speech which passes with skinheads as communication. I repeat: he was offended — so there can be no question of arguing that these are just neutral words and sounds which ought not to offend us or which can be sent to the literary dry cleaners and rehabilitated for daily use, an argument sometimes heard in the Sixties when our literature was liberated from restraints which had not made it noticeably inferior to what has since been written.

Words convey what they are intended to convey and these words are used for verbal violence which is not always disconnected from the urge for physical violence. Mr Harrison, writing out of anger, reproduced with skilful contrivance these brutal utterances with a curious rage that sometimes seems to become something almost like relish. If the purpose of poetry is to enhance understanding then the unrestraint of much of this versified reportage is not poetry. You can read it on walls all over the place. It tells you only what you know already. Still, the minority who buy and read the poem are unlikely to have their language or their spirit corrupted by it. However, it was another matter when it was decided that Mr Harrison should read it on Channel 4 late at night and that it should go into people's homes. It is not fit to be heard there, but, at least Channel 4 is able to give a warning. The real objection to the broadcast is not that the poem will corrupt viewers but that use can be made of its obscenities as a precedent in other programmes just when the BBC and IBA are trying to diminish their output of obscene language and violence. They certainly need to do so. How can parents and teachers convincingly tell the next generation not to do what Mr Harrison objects to if obscenity is authorized by television?

Yet even this is not my main point. Mr Levin feels that this is a substantial poem which should properly be heard on television and if he had explained his case by arguing that alone he would have heard nothing from me. Instead he both produced a verse with a profusion of obscenity out of context and also repeated several times a four-letter word with evident gusto, on the grounds that it should not be censored because some quite respectable people have been known to use it in restricted circumstances. He then denounced as smut-hounds or book-burners anyone who objected to the broadcast and condemned as a "campaign" the opinions of those who took this view as though his own article was not likewise part of a contrary campaign.

Thus, believing that it helped his case, he chose to victimize those who, without being silly, ignorant, or prudish, do not wish to find themselves and their families faced with obscenity on the breakfast table, in what was clearly a gratuitous taboo-breaking exercise. But who is Mr Levin to say that society may not have its taboos or to assume that people have no right to be offended by what he chooses to say because he is saying it? What good reason can there be for giving the quotation out of context in a way which actually makes it harder to justify the poem as a whole. Its only purpose must be to assert that only fools would be offended by what he chooses to write.

Mr Harrison, enraged by the graffiti of the graveyard, wrote his poem in anger and seemed to have been taken over by the words he used. Mr Levin then, without warning, presented his readers with the worst of them, outraging many just as Mr Harrison was outraged in the cemetery. It is the same offence committed against many more — and for what purpose?

Mr Levin does not seem to be arguing that this vocabulary can be cleansed of its accumulated dirt and violence. Indeed, the burden of his argument on one level is that it is offensive. But he also clearly despises anyone he thinks might be shocked and is determined that they should accept his criteria of what is sayable and writable in the context of a newspaper. But there is a difference between being shocked (who now has much shockability left?), and being offended by breaches of good manners. I can see no rational reason why we should take our notion of public good manners from Mr Levin.

THURSDAY 22 OCTOBER 1987
THE TIMES

Harrison's elegy

AREASONABLE assumption in cultural controversies is that the true source of dispute differs from the stated one. The row over D.M. Thomas's novel *The White Hotel* was less about plagiarism than about the novel's treatment of sexuality; *The Romans in Britain* at the National offended as much in its contentious history as in its nudity and buggery. The same might be said of the latest such controversy, concerning Richard Eyre's Channel 4 film of Tony Harrison's poem *v.*, now to be shown later than originally scheduled but still too early for a number of Tory MPs who, according to the *Daily Mail* ('TV FOUR LETTER POEM FURY'), are outraged that it should be shown at all. Those MPs are right to believe that the poem is shocking, but not because of its language. It shocks because it describes unflinchingly what is meant by a divided society, because it takes the abstractions we have learned to live with — unemployment, racial tension, inequality, deprivation — and gives them a kind of physical existence on the page.

DENIS BISHOP

SATURDAY 24 OCTOBER 1987
THE INDEPENDENT

in a city graveyard

Harrison wrote the poem at the time of the 1984 Miners' strike; in it he describes a return to the Leeds cemetery (situated above an old mine) where his parents lie buried. It is a flying visit, since the scholarship boy-made-good, his name in lights on Broadway, now divides his time between Newcastle, Florida and New York, but long enough to see that many of the gravestones, his parents' included, have been daubed with graffiti — the art-work of a Leeds United supporter whose aggression is expressed both in four-letter words and in the symbol 'v.', soccer shorthand for 'versus'. Harrison reflects on the other versuses of our society — divisions of class, gender, religion, language — acknowledging the vandal with the aerosol can as an *alter ego* as well as an enemy: they're one and the same 'skin' (an example of the poem's punning method), artists and wordsmiths alike.

For all its bleakness, the poem ends on a note of hope. It looks towards the moment when the 'v.' of versus might recover the meaning it had in 1945, the Churchillian 'v.' of victory, when UNITED will be not a football chant but the state of the nation.

'The language of the age is never the language of poetry', wrote an earlier elegist in a churchyard, Thomas Gray. But Wordsworth sought to make poetry speak the real language of men and so, in *v.*, does Tony Harrison, accommodating the profanities spoken daily within a verse-form that has an old-fashioned regularity of rhyme and metre.

At the end of 1984, Tony Harrison, whom I'd corresponded with but not met, sent me a draft version of *v.* What did I think? I replied as unjealously as possible that I thought it terrific — a real state-of-the nation poem. It may have taken a controversy over a TV film to bring it the wider audience it deserves, but never mind. Here it is, compulsory reading for politicians of all parties.

☐ *Blake Morrison is Literary Editor of The Observer. His latest book of poems is **The Ballad of the Yorkshire Ripper**.*

SOME READERS MAY FIND *V.*'S USE OF SEXUALLY EXPLICIT LANGUAGE OFFENSIVE

SEAN FRENCH

As I please

In fact we've just been seeing Channel Four at its independent best. As has become customary, this took the form of another public controversy, complete with the normal crowd of Tory MPs and Mrs Whitehouse. It was started by the *Daily Mail* with a front page banner headline bellowing: "FOUR-LETTER TV POEM FURY." This "torrent of four-letter filth," this "cascade of expletives," was in fact a recital of *V*, a poem by Tony Harrison, in a programme directed by Richard Eyre, who is about to take over Peter Hall's job as director of the National Theatre.

The *Mail* added that the poem was dedicated to Arthur Scargill. In fact, the reference at the beginning of the poem is not a dedication but an epigraph, a quotation from a *Sunday Times* interview with Scargill (by John Mortimer, I think): "My father still reads the dictionary every day. He says your life depends on your power to master words."

I never thought that any poet writing today could capture what was happening to Britain in so clear-eyed and unvengeful a way. But Harrison has also worked in the theatre—creating magnificent modern versions of the *Oresteia* and the medieval mystery plays—and he knows about communicating to an audience. (The two qualities don't necessarily go together.) *V* is one of the major literary products of the Thatcher years.

FRIDAY 23 OCTOBER 1987
NEW SOCIETY

BAKEWELL'S VIEW

Joan Bakewell, one of the pioneers of arts reporting on television, now commits herself to print in a weekly diary of her encounters and impressions on the cultural circuit

O N Tuesday I see the Channel 4 film of Tony Harrison's attacked poem, V: the protestors should be on his side. Harrison visits the Leeds grave of his dad and mam to find it vandalised by graffiti sprayed on by football fans taking a short cut from Leeds United. Personally, I'd have been speechless with rage and grief. Harrison is eloquent: appalled by the crudity, then thoughtful about the impoverished vocabulary, and finally generous towards frustrated lives. Isn't this the path of civilised concern?

As usual his words twist and bite. You can feel the Northern grit between his teeth, a handbeating out lines rich in things everyone enjoys such as rhymes, and rhythms and strong narrative drive. The film's images — melancholy, regretful, ironic — confirm the poem's humanity. Meanwhile, the director Richard Eyre is in the Falklands making the controversial Tumbledown. Will that too be given an unthinking blast?

SUNDAY 25 OCTOBER 1987
SUNDAY TIMES

LETTERS TO THE EDITOR

State of the art on contentious poem

From Mr S. Butterworth

Sir, The tunes which Bernard Levin pipes 'on Mondays always fall agreeably on my ears and often reach my heart. His most recent (October 19) has been an exception, but not on account of his defence of the *v* poem.

Having read the quoted extracts and learned the circumstances and the cause of their compostion (for which I thank Mr Levin for dispelling my ignorance) I was not prepared for the reasoning that several million people should attend at a Channel 4 altar and be the better off for the hearing of its recital. The four-letter words are best left where they are, in the mind, the mouth, and the locations where editors, writers and publishers legitimately exercise their freedom to express themselves as they wish.

I happen to think that universal proclamation of *v* through the employment of a *transmitter* affronts freedom and art as does much else on the screen claiming to be an expression of one or the other and which would not be thought such by any sensible person if it were broadcast through a megaphone by someone high on a ladder and/or visually portrayed.

Art does not need the mass media. Art *is* for art's sake. Could I be right in thinking that my favourite columnist had eaten something on Sunday that did not agree with him?

Yours etc,
S. BUTTERWORTH,
Aitken House,
Ridgeway Road,
Dorking, Surrey.

SATURDAY 24 OCTOBER 1987
THE TIMES

IBA members' personal standards

From the President of the National Viewers' and Listeners' Association

Sir, Mr Bernard Levin's adulation (article, October 19) of Tony Harrison's poem *v.* does at least have the virtue of bringing to the very forefront of public debate the role of Lord Thomson and the Independent Broadcasting Authority in the establishment of broadcasting standards.

The approval by the Authority of Channel 4's intended transmission of this work of singular nastiness, raises the whole question of the personal standards and judgement of its individual members. The Broadcasting Act (1981) states that "as far as possible . . . nothing is included in the programmes which offends against good taste or decency".

By agreeing to the poem's transmission the members of the Authority tell us that obscene four letter words, piled up at a speed

and with a force that magnifies their brutality, do not offend their individual standards of decency and good taste. Knowing Lord Thomson over many years, as I have, I find this difficult to believe. So is he saying that, in his judgement, the rest of us are quite happy with the transmission of language of this kind? I think we have a right to know

The televising of this poem is bound seriously to undermine public confidence in the standards and effectiveness of the IBA and gives force to the reasonable argument, not only that broadcasting should be brought under the Obscene Publications Act but that the Act itself should be made effective enough to deal with aberrations of this kind.

Yours faithfully,
MARY WHITEHOUSE,
President,
National Viewers' and Listeners' Association.

MONDAY 26 OCTOBER 1987
THE TIMES

188 *TELEVISION OBSCENITY*

Mr Gerald Howarth
Mr Anthony Coombs
Mr George Gardiner
Mr William Powell
Mr Neil Hamilton
Mr Graham Bright

★ 121

Mr Tim Janman	Mrs Ann Winterton	Mr Patrick McLoughlin
Mr Graham Riddick	Mr James Pawsey	Mr Michael Fallon
Mr Henry Bellingham	Dame Peggy Fenner	Mr Harry Greenway

This House is appalled at plans by Channel 4 to screen with the approval of the Independent Broadcasting Authority the poem 'v.' by Tony Harrison; whilst recognising that the poem may not be wholly devoid of literary merit, considers that the stream of obscenities contained in the poem is profoundly offensive and will serve to hasten the decline of broadcasting standards; and further calls on the Independent Broadcasting Authority to observe its own guidelines and instruct Channel 4 not to broadcast the poem.

As an Amendment to Mr Gerald Howarth's proposed Motion (Television Obsenity):

Mr Norman Buchan

★ 1

Line **1,** leave out 'at' to end and add 'the apparent failure of certain honourable Members to have read the poem V or, if they read it, to have understood it; points out that the whole purpose of the poem is to emphasise the real offensiveness of the obscenities referred to; and further points out that if anything is likely to hasten the decline of broadcasting standards it would be the implementation of the Peacock Report on Television and the Government Green Paper on Radio, both reportedly supported by the Prime Minister.'

Mr Roger Gale

★ 1

Line **5,** leave out from 'broadcasting' to end and insert 'futher notes that this is the latest example of the Independent Broadcasting Authority failing to create a self-regulatory framework within independent television ; and calls upon the Chairman and Director-General of the Authority, in the light of that failure, to consider their respective positions.'.

★   *The figure following this symbol gives the total number of names of Members appended, including those names added in this edition of the Notices of Questions and Motions.*

TUESDAY 27 OCTOBER 1987
HOUSE OF COMMONS
EARLY DAY MOTION

Why IBA allowed poem a hearing

From the Chairman of the Independent Broadcasting Authority

Sir, Mrs Mary Whitehouse's letter (October 26) questions the personal standards and judgement of me and the other members of the Independent Broadcasting Authority.

The programme to which she refers is an account in verse and vision by the poet Tony Harrison of a Leeds cemetery where he is distressed to find the graves of his parents and grandparents desecrated by football hooligans who use spray guns to inscribe graffiti on the tombstones. He is deeply disturbed and is moved by this experience to describe it in verse, and to seek, with poet's insight, an explanation of why these youths behave in this way.

The foul language, though frequent, is used neither to shock nor to titillate. It is an integral part of the message of the poem. It is the very reverse of gratuitous.

The members of the IBA faced a dilemma when they had to decide whether the poem was suitable for broadcasting. On the one hand there was an intensely honest poem by a poet of national reputation, and Parliament has laid on the IBA and Channel 4 the duty, in the words of the Broadcasting Act, to be distinctive, to encourage innovation and experiment and to appeal to tastes and interests not generally catered for by ITV.

On the other hand television goes freely, if not totally uninvited, into the family home. Was it consistent with the obligations of the IBA under other provisions of the Broadcasting Act to allow the broadcasting of this programme containing language that would be disturbing and offensive to a section of the viewing public?

IBA members took the unusual step of viewing the programme, and then carefully discussed the dilemma it presented. I believe it is fair to say that for each member it presented conflicting considerations not easy to reconcile. We came to the conclusion that the programme should go out on Channel 4, but late at night, when it was clearly a matter of individual choice whether or not to watch it.

We are appointed by the Home Secretary to exercise our judgement conscientiously in implementing the many provisions of broadcasting legislation including questions of taste and decency. In the case of this programme we took our decision with full regard to the responsibilities laid on us by Parliament.

Yours faithfully,
GEORGE THOMSON,
Chairman,
Independent Broadcasting Authority,
70 Brompton Road, SW3.
October 28.

THURSDAY 29 OCTOBER 1987
THE TIMES
LETTERS TO THE EDITOR

ENDPIECE

Ian Hislop

IT IS always entertaining when an attempt at censorship backfires and turns into a massive publicity campaign for the offending article. Mrs Thatcher has provided the most spectacular example of this phenomenon with the worldwide hype of *Spycatcher* but one of her backbenchers is now loyally following her example in a more modest way, with a campaign to ban Tony Harrison's poem '*v*.' from Channel Four. Gerald Howarth MP has already ensured that more people will read the poem than would ever have done before he opened his mouth, and when the televised version is shown he will be personally responsible for vastly inflating its viewing figures. Without his efforts it is unlikely that the *Independent*, worthy and comprehensive as it is, would have devoted a whole page to a two-year-old poem. There would have been no storm in the tabloids and no defences in the quality papers.

This is all to the good, not only because it makes Gerald Howarth look an idiot, but also because the poem, far from being filth, is a serious and often moving meditation of what divides people in Britain from each other. The inspiration for this was the poet finding that a skinhead football supporter had sprayed graffiti on his parents' grave, the word 'United' setting off a train of thought that was reinforced by finding the symbol 'v.' (versus) everywhere, that contradicted it. But it is the four-letter words that they wrote on the grave and that Harrison wrote in his poem that have made Mr Howarth so angry. He says that the poem 'contains a cascade of obscenities and it is ridiculous to call it art. There are apparently 47 expletives in 448 lines and as far as he is concerned that more or less concludes the case for the prosecution. It obviously does not strike him that there might be a reason for putting in the expletives and that the cascade of obscenity is sparked by the poet's own anger at seeing the words on a grave. Towards the end of the poem Harrison imagines himself in the same grave and addresses an imaginary onlooker.

'If love of art, or love gives you affront
that the grave I'm in's graffitied then, maybe,
erase the more offensive Fuck and Cunt
but leave with the worn United, one small v.'
Harrison knows the words are offensive. They offend him and he knows that they will offend others. They do, however, exist in the reality of the graveyard in Leeds and he has tried, as he shouts at an imaginary skinhead, 'to give some higher meaning to your scrawl'. As far as Mr Howarth is concerned, he has failed and the poem is not art. Why is it difficult to believe, in the words of the poem, that it is *not* 'love of art' that has given affront to this Tory MP? It is partly, I suppose, because he comes from a government notoriously unsympathetic to the arts, but more obviously because he has failed to remark on the 400 or so lines that do not contain any four-letter words (except, as Harrison remarks, the word 'poet'). Mr Howarth makes no distinction between the skinhead with the aerosol and the poet himself, and while this would probably appeal to part of Harrison who manages to identify with 'the Harpoholic Yob' at one stage of the poem, it is hardly a very intelligent reading of the words. The imaginary skinhead tells the poet 'Don't waste your breath' and mocks his attempts to find words more meaningful than the vocabulary of the aerosol. He does not like poets any more than the average backbencher: 'ah bet yer wrote a poem yer wanker you'.

Having seen a screening of the television version of the poem I predict that Mr Howarth is going to be upset by more than merely the language. There is footage of the 1984 miners' strike and even, I'm afraid, a shot of Mrs Thatcher making what appears to be a V-sign. I look forward to Mr Howarth amending his literary critique of the poem to read 'a cascade of *left-wing* obscenities', and, of course, to the subsequent even larger ratings for what would otherwise have been a typical Channel Four 'minority' offering. □

V signs

Geoff Dyer

'*WHAT IS IT that these crude words are revealing*' (From *V* by Tony Harrison).

A friend of mine who teaches literature routinely explains to his pupils why it is worth their while to attend his classes. 'When you leave here,' he says, 'two sentences of decent English will get you out of a lot of heavy situations.' In the current educational climate a more lavish justification of the humanities is, he feels, inappropriate.

As far as certain Tory MPs and the tabloid press are concerned, however, there is precious little decent in the English of a poem like Tony Harrison's *V*. It's the kind of complaint that has fuelled Harrison's efforts ever since his English teacher at Leeds Grammar interrupted his reading of Keats ('mi 'art aches . . .') with a plea for a bit more Received Pronunciation. Even his dad, from whom Harrison got the accent that appalled his teacher, greeted his first collection, *The Loiners*, with the words: '*You weren't brought up to write such mucky books.*'

The latest howls have been occasioned by the televised version of *V* in which the poet visits the family grave in Leeds and finds it sprayed with obscene graffiti. The central section of the poem is a debate between the poet and the imagined skinhead culprit ('*Who needs yer fucking poufy words? Ah write mi own.*'). The programme is a kind of poetry promo, intercutting Harrison reading the poem in a wine bar (itself the kind of irony that is bread and butter to the poet) with footage from the graveyard and its environs.

Actually composed during the miners' strike, *V* is vintage Harrison, the title punning on versus ('class v. class') and verses. Harrison was brought up in a working-class family and then 'taken' away from that background by his education; his best poems have always addressed themselves to this, the classic anguish of the scholarship boy. One of the few English poets to have a tangible sense of history, he is a product of exactly the social convulsion that first produced the Angry Young Men. His chief achievement has been to historicise

in verse an experience that has hitherto been the preserve of prose. In many ways, then, he is exactly the kind of poet the English left has always wanted.

Instead it is the right-wing press that is capitalising on him ('another probably bolshie poet', 'four letter filth', etc.). Hot on the heels of items in the media as to whether a paper like the *Star* can really be considered journalism the *Star* gets its revenge, shouting (if I can put it into Harrisonese): '*Call this fuckin' poetry?*'

Harrison has long been one of my favourite poets and the headlines in the gutter press were, for me, as depressingly mindless as were the original graffiti to Harrison. Poetry and grave were defiled by aerosol and print alike. I expect little enough from the media but, it seems, as with graffiti, there's no getting away from them. Most of the time the tabloids don't mention poetry but, as Thomas Pynchon notes somewhere (not in *V*!) we must beware of thinking of ignorance as a blank space; it has its own contours and structures, its own cohesion and logic. Since it also has a strong impulse to colonise it is no surprise that its forces should lay siege to Harrison's poem. The recent controversy is less a question of dialect versus RP than of language being suffocated by its own misuse, being forced into a space so small that it can hardly breathe.

The pressure comes not only from the guttural idiom of the tabloids but also from the sanitised clichés of respectable media-speak. Take, for example, Michael Buerk's recent look back at his time in South Africa in which an abundance of TV footage was squandered by Buerk's inability to break through the bland idiom of BBC reportage. Freed from the strictures of the news bulletin he filled up the extra space with the echoing of empty rhetoric about 'evil in the heart of man'.

Ostensibly there may be little in common between Buerk and the language of the tabloids; the important point is that, equally incapable of bearing the weight of contemporary reality, both flatten and impoverish words even as they use them. *V*, for all its flaws — the expediencies of rhyme and rhythm with which Harrison extricates himself from the tight corners of the quatrain — shows linguistic vigour and poetry fighting for their lives. The odds against them are such that it is only natural to butt, slash and gouge. □

FRIDAY 30 OCTOBER 1987
NEW STATESMAN

Four and against

BLESSING the transmission by Channel 4 this coming Wednesday night of Tony Harrison's poem "v" is one of the easier decisions the Independent Broadcasting Authority has taken this year.

The poem is full of four-letter words usually found on walls but, in this case, sprayed on the gravestones of the poet's parents in Leeds by supporters of Leeds United. His sense of outrage led to the poem.

Whether "v" achieves its artistic purpose is a matter of opinion. Mr Harrison uses the four-letter expletives contrapuntally, first as they appear on the stones, then in an imagined dialogue between himself and the United vandals. He wants to express all the antagonisms which he sees in a disunited Britain: North v South, male v female, young v old. For my taste, a poem should not have to explain its meaning, and the line "These vs are all the ver-suses of life" is as jarring as a glimpse of the strapless bra beneath the ballgown.

But the poem is a serious work of art. It was not written to appeal to prurient interests and it is not to be broadcast anywhere near the nine o'clock watershed at which good children are supposed to shut their ears and eyes. Politicians who call the poem "a torrent of filth" and "packed with obscenity" know more about getting headlines in the *Daily Mail* than about writing poems.

For the broadcasting authorities, far harder decisions have to be taken about milder coarse language in family viewing times. I am much more unhappy about the way these are going. The BBC condones, for example, the use of "piss off" and "pain in the arse" in "Bread", which goes out on Sunday evenings at 8.35pm. That fine writer Carla Lane says she is not writing "words"; she is writing the way people in Liverpool talk; and with a string of television successes going back to "The Liver Birds" behind her, no one would want to stop her doing her stuff.

All the same, realism does not require her scripts for family viewing-time to contain what is called in the telly trade "the F-word", although it is common enough in Liverpool and everywhere else. Art is not a mirror

On Wednesday at 11pm Tony Harrison's controversial film-poem "v" will be shown on C 4. BRENDA MADDOX reports

or microphone held up to nature. It is always selective, and realistic dialogue is never anything like as inarticulate and repetitive as real speech – a point made by the Harrison poem. People who swear do so not once in a half-hour but every minute, interspersed with "ums" and "I means" and other brakes on dramatic tension which never reach the screen. Social comedy and satire would lose none of their force if the authorities demanded cleaner language before nine o'clock, and then allowed a far freer rein later at night. Why bleep "The Deer Hunter"?

In no way do the BBC or the IBA treat swearing lightly. Indeed, BBC policy is that all four-letter words must be "referred upwards" – that is, they cannot be transmitted

without the permission of higher authority. And as for the F-word, it must go to the very highest: the managing director, television. A nice Christmas present for Mr Bill Cotton would be a modified version of Harry Truman's famous desk sign "The Buck Stops Here".

One other word requires similar treatment: the C-word. This, however, is still so taboo that it hardly ever reaches the air, even in films late at night. Its liberal use in "v" is probably the real reason for the current storm.

I do not think for a minute that the broadcasting authorities are the wrong arbiters on such matters. They are far better placed than the new Broadcasting Standards Council to make the unending decisions on realism v decency, preserv-

Tony Harrison: prompted by outrage

ing standards v moving with the times. Neither television nor dramatists can be restricted to a fossilised language while everybody else is speaking in a different way. The procedure will never be simple or satisfy everybody.

Crude blacklists of forbidden words lend themselves to ridicule. So do publicly-issued "rules". In Washington the Federal Communications Commission has announced a crackdown on dirty words on radio. So can we go ahead with our annual reading of Molly Bloom's filthy soliloquy from James Joyce's *Ulysses?* asked the Pacific Foundation (always

bruising for a fight on obscenity).

The FCC wisely held its tongue rather than be seen to ban a book which a federal judge in 1933 ruled to be not obscene. The case, as Commissioner James Quello noted, "would have been a tough putt, legally".

Recent research by both the IBA and Channel 4 show that people in Britain are far more disturbed by bad language on the box than by sex and violence. Public opinion is right. Most of us are not influenced by what we see on television: fantasy action, pictures in a box. But words pass the video bar-

rier. They are the currency of our lives. It is wrong to pretend that they do not exist out of context. They do. Like coins, they have recognised value. Like ammunition, they explode, regardless of where they are.

Realism about language on television requires a recognition that swear words have magical power. They refer to the processes of procreation and excretion, or in the words of one academic, "the portals of existence".

The debate on television sex and violence has been misplaced. As the public well understands, the word's the thing.

A note on the poem

DERWENT MAY writes: Is "v" a good poem ? That seems the important question. If it's very good, that makes the case for allowing it to be broadcast a strong one. If it's a bad poem, or an uninteresting one, then the obscenities must certainly be added to the low quality as an additional reason for not broadcasting it.

In my view, it's an unhealthy poem, in the sense that it seems to emerge from a rather disturbed and unpleasant state of mind. Tony Harrison finds his parents' graves covered with graffiti. He is enraged; all the same, he wants to understand the drunken football fans who have desecrated the Leeds cemetery in this way.

Unfortunately, all his thoughts are really about himself, not about them. Throughout the poem he boasts that he is a poet, living in a far larger world than his family and

former schoolboy friends. But he also feels guilty about this improvement in his circumstances. This is why he tries to stretch his imagination back into his earlier life, and understand again the milieu in which these foul-mouthed yobbos still live.

However, this effort gets him nowhere worth going. For he neither allows himself plainly to judge the yobbos by his new standards, and assert the genuine superiority of those standards; nor does he accept that the yobbos have a right to their own ideas and feelings. Either response would show some respect for the yobbos. But he is not really concerned with them at all.

What he wants somehow to do is embrace them and claim that his comprehensive soul contains both them and the new person he has become. This is where the obscene words come

in. He is showing both his new-found literary friends and the yobbos that he can swear and shock as disgustingly as anybody – that in this way he is bigger than any of them. And the obscenity seems also meant to shock the readers – to show them the same thing, and make them feel worried and inferior. (Of course, some unhappy critics and readers like feeling that.)

Harrison's use of language, his deft rhythms and rhymes, all make this a genuinely effective poem. But the epigraph from Arthur Scargill – "My father still reads the dictionary every day. He says your life depends on your power to master words" – is perhaps more apt than the poet knows. Harrison, like Scargill, is using his skill with words to impose a private fantasy on his listeners, not to elicit a hard, pure truth.

Censorship : Let

DAVID GLENCROSS argues that TV should have
the same freedom as newspapers and the cinema.

TELEVISION has magical powers, causing those who watch it to suspend judgment and abandon any sense of personal responsibility for what they do. If only, for example, the TV weather forecasters had correctly predicted the hurricane, then it would not have happened, believe some. Others assert that school truancy and work absenteeism are the result of some ITV companies broadcasting through the night.

Then there are four-letter words, undeleted expletives. When an extract from Tony Harrison's poem 'v.' containing these words is printed in *The Times*, embedded in an article by Bernard Levin, the social fabric of the nation survives. The *Times* is, after all, a family newspaper (its sister and brother being the *Sun* and the *News of the World*) left around the houses of literate families at times when precocious children could be expected to explore its contents.

A few days later the *Independent* prints the poem in full with an introduction from Blake Morrison, *The Observer's* Literary Editor. Society remains intact.

But when the poem is read by its author on Wednesday at 11.00 p.m. on Channel 4 it will be a very different cup of tea. Hordes of impressionable and allegedly semi-literate viewers, previously exposed only to the delicate sensibilities of the tabloid press, will be instantly corrupted by this ' obscene filth masquerading as literature.' Such viewers must be presumed to have no knowledge of the offending words.

It is in the hope of combating this kind of confusion about television's role and function that broadcasters must sincerely wish that Mrs Mary Whitehouse or one of her acolytes will be invited to serve on the proposed Broadcasting Standards Council.

On the assumption that its composition will be broadly based, rather than the vanguard for any particular section of opinion, all those who serve on it will be obliged to listen to the views of those who differ from them. That should be a valuable educational experience for any who believe that television is the be all and end all of people's lives.

The only people for whom it has that importance are the people who work in it. The public as a whole, as the most recent findings of the Broadcasting Research Unit illustrate, are quite able to make choices as to what they will watch, wish others to exercise their own freedom of choice, and resent the activities of those who claim to speak on their behalf.

This is not to say that there should be a torrent of four-letter words on television just to show how liberal it can be. It is precisely because there is no list of forbidden words that the use of the

the viewers decide

most extreme language should be considered most carefully whenever the issue arises. It is precisely because no definite proof exists, or is likely to exist, of a connection between on-screen violence and violence in real life that broadcasters do need to take care in the way that they portray violence and the times at which it is shown.

It is strange though that the proposed Broadcasting Standards Council looks unlikely to be widened to cover cinema or the Press. It seems that those who have such anxiety about the portrayal of sex and violence are unacquainted with what is on offer at their local cinemas and choose to avert their eye when passing their newsagents. Doubtless this will all be remedied as the legislation passes through Parliament. If this remedy is applied, then the council could have a valuable role in distinguishing the relative merits and effects of all national, though presumably not international media.

Given that the name of the new body is the Broadcasting Standards Council, and not the Broadcasting Complaints Council, it would be reasonable to assume that it will consider representations from those members of the public, who do not share the view that television is on an unending downward spiral and who accept that there is more than one legitimate view about many controversial programmes. A body which considers only complaints will get a very distorted picture of the way television is generally regarded.

It is true that the existing Broadcasting Complaints Commission does only consider complaints, but this is because its remit is to deal only with specific allegation of unfair treatment and unjustified invasions of privacy. It can only entertain complaints from those who are directly involved or identified in a programme.

Home Office Minister Timothy Renton has recently been on a fact-finding visit to North America. The Americans have held up their hands in horror at what they consider to be undue British sensitivity on violence, especially on hearing of the IBA's decision to reduce foreign material in peak-time. In return the Americans have expressed themselves shocked by British television's treatment of sex. The mid-Atlantic consummation in ' Brideshead Revisited ' was thought to be especially daring.

Other Americans have put it about that they find it hard to understand why British television is being harried with quite so much vigour. They had believed that vendettas were confined to Sicily. Could it be that television's very independence is so distrusted ?

The answer might be to expose our legislators to a week of American television or Australian television or any country's television that they choose. Then, like the vast majority of their fellow citizens, they would de-mystify television. Here be not demons, but words and pictures. Why not trust the people to use them as such ?

David Glencross is director of television at the IBA. He writes in a personal capacity.

LETTERS TO THE EDITOR

Reading of 'v'

From Viscount Tonypandy

Sir, Lord Thomson, Chairman of the Independent Broadcasting Authority (October 29), has failed to answer adequately the letter from Mrs Mary Whitehouse (October 26). He maintains that the foul language in Mr Harrison's peom, though frequent, is used neither to shock nor to titillate.

Quite clearly the foul language *has* shocked and it is no excuse for the IBA to dismiss the complaint airily by stating

We came to the conclusion that the programme should go out on Channel 4, but late at night, when it was clearly a matter of individual choice whether or not to watch it.

Regardless of the timing when a programme is broadcast, it is a matter of individual choice whether or not to watch it. Until a programme has been watched one cannot tell what it will contain.

Surely the IBA can fulfil their obligation "to be distinctive, to encourage experiment and to appeal to tastes and interests not generally catered for by ITV" without approving the broadcasting of foul language such as that to

which Mrs Whitehouse has justifiably taken exception.

It is no answer to say

In the case of this programme we took our decision with full regard to the responsibilities laid on us by Parliament.

We have a right to expect every decision by the IBA to take into account the responsibilities laid on them by Parliament. Foul language is offensive on the television at any hour. We look to the IBA to protect proper standards. Well done, Mary Whitehouse.

Yours faithfully,
GEORGE TONYPANDY,
House of Lords.

MONDAY 2 NOVEMBER 1987
THE TIMES

Obscenity v. poetry

Dear Sir,
Ever since last Saturday I have been trying to guess the reasons which prompted you to publish the 112 verses of Mr Harrison's doggerel in your paper. I, for one, did not expect you to share the editorial judgement of Channel 4. Of course everyone knows these words — who could fail to who watches TV? We have come a long way since London audiences were shocked by Eliza Doolittle's "bloody". It proved to be the top of a slippery slope; and whether the moral climate today is more "civilised" than it was in 1911 is at least questionable.

Everyone who so wishes can buy and read Mr Harrison's poems and form their own conclusions; but you must know, Sir, that they offend very many people in all walks of life (Mr Harrison himself seems to have found them offensive) and good manners alone (which may not "make men" but are simply evidence of consideration for others) should surely prevent their gratuitous display to all and sundry.

Sincerely,
Sir GILBERT LONGDEN
London, SW7

Dear Sir,
It would be interesting to know the real motivation behind your publication (24 October) of the whole of Tony Harrison's *v*.

Was it a carefully calculated manifestation of the campaign to render meaningless the Government's intention to bring broadcasting under the Obscene Publications Act? Was the power of this pressure so great that the reputation of *The Independent*, itself, as a newspaper of real quality fit for the family breakfast table, became of little or no consequence?

So why should anyone bother? It seems to me a matter more of aesthetics than morality — except in so far as an unsolicited affront can always raise moral issues. The four letter word, referring as it does to sexual intercourse has within its very sound, let alone context, a harshness, even brutality, that negates and destroys the nature of the love, sensitivity and commitment which is or should be, its very essence.

To accept and normalise such language is to provide, at best, the cheap and easy option. The intrinsic message behind your publication of the poem is that the concepts of the increasingly outdated permissive humanism are more important to you than

the enlightened courtesy which you owe to your readers.

Yours faithfully,
MARY WHITEHOUSE
President
National Viewers' and Listeners' Association

Dear Sir,
It is unfortunate that the respectable fetish of "bad language" prevents two of your readers (letters, 28 October) from seeing what is going on in Tony Harrison's brilliant poem, *v*.

The poem recognises that the language is offensive, not least to the poet himself whose parents' grave is desecrated. He does not revert to the easy indignation expressed in the letters. Instead, he attempts the more challenging task of understanding the complex and terrible divisions in the present new order, and does not evade the violent language in which those divisions are expressed.

The moralising of F. H. Johnson and N. C. Flamee and the far more pernicious attempts of certain Tory MPs to prevent the broadcast of the poem, are not a substitute for the moving understanding which the poem presents. Yet again, objections to "obscenity" are being used by our rulers to prevent recognition of the devastation over which they are presiding.

Yours sincerely,
IAN MURRAY
St Albans, Hertfordshire

MONDAY 2 NOVEMBER 1987
THE INDEPENDENT

LETTERS TO THE EDITOR

Poetry critics with tin ears

Dear Sir,
I would like to congratulate you on publishing Tony Harrison's poem, *v*. The protests which it has aroused indicate quite clearly that the protesters have not taken the trouble to read it carefully, if at all. Harrison's indictment of what they call bad language is far more passionate and intelligent than their own. Anyone who can de-

scribe as doggerel this fine, thoughtful and metrically accomplished poem must have a tin ear. One may not like Harrison's work, but one cannot dismiss it as incompetent.
Yours sincerely,
MARGARET DRABBLE
London, NW3

Dear Sir,
Tony Harrison's elegy in an urban churchyard is a vision of Charity broader and higher than Mrs

Whitehouse's narrow obsessions would allow.
In it, the communion of souls seeks to embrace the mindless vandal even in terms of his own verbal poverty.
Congratulations on publishing, in this eloquent, witty and passionate sermon, such unfashionably high-toned family breakfast reading.
TOM PHILLIPS ARA
Royal Academy
London, SW1

TUESDAY 3 NOVEMBER 1987
THE INDEPENDENT

Thoughtful 'v.'

Dear Sir,
Thank you for making available Tony Harrison's *v.*, one of the most interesting, studious, thoughtful and craftsmanlike po-

ems to be published in England since Philip Larkin's *Church Going*.
As Thomas Hardy noted before *Jude*: " 'Never retract. Never explain. Get it down and let them howl.' Words said to Jowett by a

very practical friend."
Yours sincerely,
Dr EDWARD BLACK
Department of Language Studies
The London School
of Economics
London, WC2

WEDNESDAY 4 NOVEMBER 1987
THE INDEPENDENT

Classics helped author of 'v'

From the President of the Classical Association of Great Britain

Sir, I was sorry to have been out of the country and to have missed what appear to have been lively discussions on the future of classics. I was glad, therefore, to have returned in time to read the letter from Mr Hector Thomson (October 31) affirming the central role of Latin in the continuity of English literature.

While I should like to remind him that English literature did not come to an end with T. S. Eliot, a

former president of this association, I am very glad to be able to endorse all he said by swearing, if I may be permitted, that without the many years I spent acquiring Latin and Greek I should never have been able to compose my poem *v*.
Yours faithfully,
TONY HARRISON, President,
The Classical Association of Great Britain,
c/o Department of Classics,
University College, Cardiff,
PO Box 78,
Cardiff, South Glamorgan.

TUESDAY 3 NOVEMBER 1987
THE TIMES

69

CHANNEL FOUR TELEVISION
Duty Officers' Report

A complete log of phone calls about v. made by public and press to Channel Four on Wednesday 4 November 1987, from 11.29 a.m. The entries are taken verbatim from the logs of four duty officers manning the switchboard when the Channel Four film of v. was shown. Only the names and telephone numbers of the callers have been deleted.

WEDNESDAY 4 NOVEMBER:

11.29. Male caller furious about the 4-letter words in this prog. Calmed down when explained in context and thanked C4 for being patient and listening to him.

XX.XX. Mrs F. Complaining about the plan to tx: what will young teenagers think, you aren't allowed to put this sort of thing in the newspapers so why is it on TV. Advised that V had been published in full in the Independent. Caller rang off.

XX.XX. A Dorset village represented by Mrs C would like to register their disappointment that C4 are going ahead with this, unforgivable, and also a great great pity. We are very much against this.

15.05. Mrs C (Harpenden). I really do object to this being shown at all, especially with the very strong language.

21.27. Newcastle Journal enquiring if they could ring back at 11.30 for audience response. Advised to contact Press Office tomorrow morning.

22.24. Dr M (Nottingham) calling to say he is very glad we're showing this as it is a very important piece of work.

23.00. [*Film starts*]

23.15. Mr T (London). Fantastic programme.

23.20. Mr R complaining of the bad language. Would not leave name or no. 'Mouthing obscene language.'

23.20. Mr H (Ipswich). Stupid idiotic foul language. Born and bred in a mining village. Surely nobody wants to hear this tripe. Isn't there enough sadness in the world without showing this?

23.21. Mrs S (Liverpool). Disgusting programme.

23.22. Mr B (Salisbury). Can't believe what he's seeing or hearing. Is there a lunatic loose? Disgusting language. Foul. Terrible. We don't live in this bad a world. No value in the programme. V unpleasant.

23.22. Anon male to say this is totally disgusting. Feels it is not correct to show this at any time of day.

23.23. Mr S to say this is totally disgusting rubbish.

23.25. Mr F (Dane End), 'foul language unnecessary and obscene'.

23.25. Mr B, regular viewer of C4 who was astounded by this having been shown. It's disgusting.

23.26. Mr I (London), 'language filthy and should not have been on'.

23.27. Mr E (Whitby). This is brilliant, he hit the nail right on the head. Gave details of book. Went on to say how much he enjoyed Equinox and all C4 programmes in general.

23.29. Mr S (London), 'disgusted with the content'. Would like to know who was responsible.

23.30. Mr W (wdn't leave phone no). Patronising towards young people and offensive. Not v good.

23.31. Jack Bell from the Daily Mirror transferred to Press Office.

23.32. Mr Y (London). Thanks for having the courage to show it. V. good.

23.34. Ms M (Nottingham). Excellent. Haven't seen anything like that before. Brilliant. V interesting.

23.35. [Film ends]

23.35. Ms W (Maidenhead). Particularly boring. He's not a very good poet. But, are we going to have more poetry on? Do to follow up.

23.35. Mr H (London), 'best prog he has ever seen and the so-called "obscene language" was totally necessary to the content of the poem'.

23.36. Mr G (London). Terrific for putting that on. Wonderful.

23.37. Ms D (London). Absolutely wonderful. Can't bear bad language but thought this was brilliant.

23.39. Ms D (Nottingham), to say she was very glad this was shown.

23.40. Mr G (London). Never rung a TV company before in his life. Best production he's seen in ten years.

23.40. Mr M (London): thank you for showing this 'excellent prog'.

23.40. Mr G (London), to say how much he enjoyed it.

23.41. Mr A (hospital doctor, London). Wonderful and more programmes like it please.

23.41. Mr D (London) 'thanking the producer for showing this excellent prog'.

23.42. Mrs R (London), congratulations on this marvellous programme. It's wonderful; one of the most wonderful programmes I've ever seen.

23.43. Mr & Mrs H (London). How much we appreciated the programme. Excellent. More please.

23.43. Caller (wishing to remain anonymous) thanking us for showing this prog and cannot wait to go out and buy Tony Harrison's book.

23.43. Mr F (Leeds), thoroughly good thing you broadcast this.

23.44. Mr M (London). Enjoyed it. Thank you for showing it.

23.45. Mr G (London) thanking us for showing this programme.

23.45. Female. Brilliant, well filmed and presented.

23.46. Mr S (Nottingham) thanked us for showing this prog. Particularly due to the campaign in the press to undermine C4.

23.47. Mr P (London) 'commends C4 and the production team for this prog'.

23.47. Tom S, who is still at school, and doesn't take much interest in poetry to say this was really good. Gave details of book.

23.48. Mr R (Cumnock). Bad language. Didn't appreciate it.

23.49. Caller thanking us for showing the prog.

23.50. Mr W (London). V courageous and brave to broadcast it. Extremely interesting and very impressed.

23.51. Mr R (Bishops Stortford), amazed at how good this was. Marvellous poem and he is irritated by all the people who complain without listening properly.

23.58. Mr S (London). Thank you for broadcasting it. Illuminated the poem brilliantly. Congratulations and don't let the carpers put you off doing more of this sort of thing.

THURSDAY 5 NOVEMBER

00.00. Mr E (Norwich) 'thoroughly enjoyed prog and requesting to know audience response. Advised unable to give this info.

00.02. Mr C (Nottingham), thought it was very good. Felt (as did many of the previous callers) that in view of the amount of bad press he should cast his vote in favour and 'stand up and be counted'.

00.02. Mr S (London), 'congratulating us for showing the prog'.

00.05. Ms M (London) 'was appalled by scurrilous press and was very impressed we stuck to our guns and tx an excellent prog'.

00.31. Mr K (Wangford), 'very strong and powerful – politicians should address their energies into the social problems featured in the poem and not to whether C4 should have tx it'.

00.36. Four more callers all appreciative.

10.09. Mr C (Leamington Spa). Found the language foul and unnecessary, Strongly objects to it.

10.20. Mrs H (Leominster). This was so beautiful and moving. Riveting and read so well.

10.47. Female caller in reception for details of book. Thought prog was very good – poetry book would make good Christmas present.

11.44. Lengthy call from anon female shouting about that awful man saying C.U.N.T. and F.U.C.K., which she repeated, again and again. He was a right trouble maker, you can tell how rotten he was. In her day people were brought up properly.

13.06. Ms C (teacher, Nottingham) thought prog was really exceptional but should be screened earlier in evening for her students.

13.36. Female caller wishing to write to Tony Harrison advised to write c/o C4.

14.45. Mr H (London). 'I knew the poem before of course, but the visual image gave it so much more power, I am very grateful to Channel Four for showing it.'

15.25. Video request, dealt with.

16.10. Mr B (London): Tony Harrison ought to be in a mental home, disgusting to think that this was on, absolute pornography, it wasn't even poetry, he's no poet, that man looked sick, he'll be in that grave with his parents soon enough, it was on LBC this morning and they were pipping out all the swear words, and all you could hear was pip, pip, pip, Channel 4 just feed the nation on left-wing propaganda, anyway I don't want to talk to a minion like you, I want to talk to Programme Planning. Refused to transfer caller, who subsequently rang off.

21.00. Mr W (London). I have just finished watching V on my video, and I am so moved the tears are running down my cheeks still, so full of compassion, most moved, please accept my deepest appreciation.

PUBLIC RESPONSE TO 'V'

'Before transmission, the IBA received 32 letters expressing concern about the decision to show *v.* Seventeen were from Conservative MPs and one from a Liberal MP. The majority of these appeared to have been prompted by a letter sent by Mary Whitehouse who had written to them on 16 October 1987, alerting them to the fact that the programme was to be broadcast and enclosing a photocopy of two pages of the poem. A further 16 letters were received from people writing in their capacity as individual viewers; 14 expressed concern and 2 were congratulatory.

The level of public response to the transmission of *v.* was relatively low. The flood of public protest expected was not realised. In contrast to the pre-transmission post bag (34 letters), 6 letters were received after the programme was transmitted; 4 were from complainants (including 2 MPs) and 2 were congratulatory. Most comment was received by telephone calls, mainly direct to Channel 4 on the night of transmission or on the day immediately following. The majority of these were in favour of its transmission.'

From *Why did we broadcast v.? A case study on how the IBA made its decision, and how the public responded* (Independent Broadcasting Authority, 1988).

TV Mail

□ ALL the fuss about the poetry reading last night by Tony Harrison of his scatological poem V (C4) would never have occurred if Jeremy Isaacs, with hand on heart, had been able to swear that his station was a regular patron of poetry.

In fact, one of its greatest omissions has been its failure to develop anything on the lines of Radio 4's Poetry Please. It is not surprising, therefore, that Mr Isaacs should find himself under attack for suddenly defending the rights of poets against the Philistines, when the object he is defending is the heavily flawed V.

But the critics also expose themselves to criticism. V was no deliberate shocker, but a serious, if ponderous, cry of pain against the wilful vandalism of the gravestones in a Leeds churchyard, including those of Harrison's parents and grandparents.

The poem was overlong and tackled too wide a range of discontents. Without losing any four-letter words, its message could have been better conveyed in a fifth of the time.

THURSDAY 5 NOVEMBER 1987
DAILY MAIL

Why Mary washes whiter . .

□ HOW secure I feel to know that responsible adults like Mary Whitehouse are looking out for our moral protection.

You may have thought Tony Harrison's recital of his poem "V" on Channel 4 last Wednesday was a sensitive and brave piece of TV.

You were wrong. Thank heavens for Mary. Even without watching it, she can assure us it is a "string of four letter words". Even more astonishing is her reaction to last week's Des O'Connor show featuring Jim Davidson.

Yes, we all thought Davidson's "jokes" about his imaginary black friend Chalky, who uses a blow pipe in his duties as bus conductor, were disgusting, racist and deeply offensive.

But not a peep from Mary or her watchdog chums, so obviously that was "good family viewing". Glad someone is keeping us straight.

SUNDAY 8 NOVEMBER 1987
SUNDAY MIRROR
MURIEL GRAY COLUMN

---

v are not amused

MOST OVER PUBLICISED event of the week was the poem-film v (C4), which turned out to be a literal-minded video for the literary-minded. Tony Harrison recited his expletives-packed "We are all guilty" impressions of a society which breeds vandals who drink Harp lager, to a politely agonised assembly of people sipping white wine and orange juice.

The magic of director Richard Eyre's television imagery managed only to transform Harrison's "pensioner in a tur-ban" into a picture of an Asian in a hat. Even with Pat Gavin's graphics the programme proved conclusively that most poetry is rendered prosaic by visual illustration.

A far more disgusting TV event was the sight of Jonathan King in an ermine bikini.

SUNDAY 8 NOVEMBER 1987
SUNDAY TELEGRAPH
CHRISTOPHER TOOKEY COLUMN

74

THE VEXED QUESTION OF CENSORSHIP

Tony Harrison (left) provoked strong reactions from Mrs Mary Whitehouse (centre) and Gerald Howarth MP (right) with his poem, V.

CHRISTOPHER FREW thinks we should be very worried about the growing censorship movement in the wake of reactions to Tony Harrison's controversial poem, V.

CHANNEL 4 last week broadcast a film of Tony Harrison reading his poem, V.

The publicity it was given was due not to the quality of the poem itself or to Harrison's status as translator of the Oresteia and adapter of the Mysteries for the National Theatre, but to the fact that the poem contained most of the monosyllabic English swearwords.

It was consequently, "a torrent of filth," according to the Daily Mail, and "a cascade of obscenities," according to Gerald Howarth MP. Mary Whitehouse wrote to the Home Secretary, demanding the resignation of Lord Thomson, chairman of the IBA.

The absurdity of these attacks and the predictable behaviour of the stock characters may lull us into a benign tolerance: we've heard it before, we'll surely hear it again. But I think it's more serious, and certainly more depressing, than that.

First, briefly, the poem itself. It is set in a cemetery in Leeds where Harrison, visiting his parents' grave, notices the graffiti sprayed on the gravestones. The swearwords, defiling the memorials to the dead, are the point of departure for Harrison's ruminations on the physical and mental wasteland of the industrial north-east, and on the power of language side by side with inarticulateness.

Amateurs of smut, filth, and moral turpitude may remember Mr Howarth

SATURDAY 14 NOVEMBER 1987
GLASGOW HERALD

as the sponsor of a Bill in the last Parliament to amend the Obscene Publications Acts. The Bill would have brought television within the scope of the Acts and changed the test of obscenity to whatever "a reasonable person would regard as grossly offensive." The Bill fell for lack of time, but there is every reason to suppose it will be revived, not least Mr Howarth's prominence in the present affair.

I think we may assume that Mr Howarth regards himself. as a reasonable person and the poem V, as grossly offensive. It would follow, then, that Harrison, the London Review of Books (where the poem first appeared), Penguin Books (Selected Poems), and Channel 4 should be prosecuted — and convicted. Lord Thomson would not, of course, have survived the showing of Scum.

The repression involved in that little scenario is one aspect of the matter, but equally disturbing is the militant philistinism which it illustrates, the assault on the value of language and the rigour of logic. To misunderstand, or misrepresent, the function and context of the swearwords in V indicates an aesthetic sterility which is becoming ever more dominant in the debate of public issues.

If the Howarth and Whitehouse strain of intellectual vandalism is unappealing, its growing incorporation into law should be a cause of alarm and considerably more robust reaction than has so far been demonstrated.

The imbecilic reaction to V is at once a microcosm of a wider malaise and a detail in a planned incursion into artistic and media freedom.

Denunciation of the evils of video and television has fallen into a pattern of what might be called the forced convergence of parallel lines, deducing causation where only coincidence can be demonstrated. On the one hand, football riots, rising crime rate, increasing violence; on the other, video, television; therefore, the one is caused by the other. What some might call the symptoms are "proved" to be the disease.

The most recent example of this deduction from parallels was after the Hungerford massacre. Before the first victims had been buried, Mrs Whitehouse was on television with all the controlled zest of a professional mourner, quoting unnamed reports to sustain her thesis that television was to blame. It was not a performance easily associated with the Christian virtues she so warmly accords herself.

And what was the evidence to support the guilt theory of television? The significant fact about the post-Hungerford analysis was that no newspaper (and how some must have tried!) could find evidence to show that Ryan had been unnaturally addicted to violent television or to video nasties.

The horror of Hungerford was precisely the absence of cause; but that could not be borne, and so television was lynched.

Predictable in the present state of the tabloids, this "link" was an appalling abdication of responsibility by the quality press, and the repetition which made the connection seem respectable was in fact the more reprehensible in the absence of any evidence to prove, or even plausibly to suggest, such a theory.

If this was an aberration on the part of the press, it forms a consistent part of the repertoire of publicity tricks employed by whitehouse (I use the lower case in a generic sense). The most intense and successful example of the whitehouse strategy was the video nasties' campaign which culminated in the Video Recordings Act 1984. That campaign repays study if we are reastically to anticipate what Mr Howarth's remarks and his Bill portend.

In early 1982 the trade body, the British Videogram Association (BVA), worried by the emphasis on violence in advertisements for a number of video titles, referred the advertisements to the Advertising Standards Authority. At about the same time, the BVA asked the British Board of Film Censors (BBFC) to set up a working party to review the problem of these violent videos and to recommend a system of classification.

The BBFC remains a voluntary body in respect of cinema film classification, and the BVA envisaged a similar code in respect of video, to be enforced by the industry. It is clear that the video industry itself was early aware of the problem of the nasties and took prompt and responsible action.

The Government at this point were keeping their distance. Asked in the Commons in October 1982 if legislation were envisaged to impose video classification, Christopher Mayhew referred to the projected BVA/BBFC report and added: "Should such a scheme be introduced, we would wish to assess its effect before deciding whether any statutory controls were required."

It is a measure of the political effectiveness of the whitehouse campaign that, within 18 months, a perniciously worded Bill was on its triumphant way through Parliament in an atmosphere such that anyone voicing any reservation its wording or consequences was howled down as a champion of porn if not a corrupter of children.

Mrs Whitehouse, supported by the tabloids, most notably the Mail, usurped the concern shown by the BVA, and by late 1982 the campaign to amplify and 'distort the nasties' influence was under way. Every evil under the sun was attributed to their pervasive influence, and video as a whole took on some of the scapegoat qualities once attributed to Original Sin.

The single most potent element of the campaign was the allegation that children were put at risk. Authority for this assumption was the speciously named Parliamentary Group Video Enquiry, which purported to show that over 40% of under-sevens had seen at least one video nasty.

This report was published to coincide with the second reading of the Video Recording Bill, and effectively precluded rational debate, providing "evidence" against which it was impossible to argue. The report was, as one of the group said, "exactly what we wanted."

It was only after the "debate" had been won that doubts began to surface. Significant was the fact that the "Parliamentary Group" had no parliamentary status whasoever. Not irrelevant was the fact that the Methodist and Roman Catholic churches, originally co-opted to support the inquiry, formally disassociated themselves from the report.

Precisely to the point was the fact that the Oxford Polytechnic Television Research Unit, commissioned to carry out the research on which the report was to be based, had, the week before its publication, repudiated the framework, context, and conclusions of the report.

The head of the unit, the Rev. Brian Brown, based his denunciation on the not unreasonable ground that he had seen a copy of the report — with its conclusions — written before any of his unit's data was available· blanks had been left where the data were to appear. It is not surprising that the report was exactly what they wanted.

Sceptical towards the abnormally high incidence of video nasty penetration alleged in the report, a separate academic group prepared a second questionnaire, based on the PGVE original but including invented titles of lurid nature as well as genuine titles. As a result of the survey, 68% of the children questioned claimed to have seen a video nasty which *did not exist*. On such rigorous evidence was the Video Recordings Act driven into law.

Two further veterans of the video campaign lie quiescent, awaiting revival in the drive for a more stringent Obscene Publications Act. First, the paradoxical combination of parental concern and parental ineptitude. Those who accept without question that "you can't stop children seeing the stuff" are the same pillars of society who call for oppressive legislation to compensate for their spectacular inadequacy.

Second is the implication of the insidious little phrase in 4(1) of the Video Recordings Act, where classification is to have "special regard to the likelihood of video works . . . being viewed in the home." That phrase, inserted at a late stage, provides justification for a stricter video classification than for the cinema version. Where the privacy of the home was once the cornerstone of family values, it is now draped in the most ominous implications.

It is taking account of these underlying assumptions, as well as his keen critical faculty, that we should observe Mr Howarth's reappearance as champion of virtue and likely sponsor of a revived Bill.

It seems simple: what a "reasonable person" would find grossly offensive. David Mellor, Home Office Minister at the time of Howarth's first attempt, foresaw no problem: "A reasonable person can tell the difference between trash and art." But what constitutes a reasonable person? Mr Howarth and Mrs Whitehouse? Or Jeremy Isaacs and Michael Grade? Are they mutually exclusive or inscrutably harmonious?

Mr Mellor was confident that the courts would solve the problem: "There are quite a number of people who are trying to pollute our society with unacceptable filth. But for too long the courts have been inhibited from making a sensible decision." Not only reasonable now, but sensible.

What Mr Mellor meant, and the video campaign bore him out, was that when prosecutions were brought under the existing law, juries refused, with irritating regularity, to convict, even though numerous attempts were made. The Evil Dead, for example, was subject to 40 separate pieces of litigation, a "quite lamentable situation" in the opinion of the judge who roundly criticised the Director of Public Prosecutions, while awarding full costs against him. Most unsatisfactory.

The spate of seizures, prosecutions, and intimidation at the height of the nasties' hysteria brought the law into disrepute, and the subjective terms of the proposed amendment would have exactly the same effect.

Howarth and Whitehouse assured Channel 4 of increased viewing for their programme, to the benefit of poetry, but we should beware lest that turn out to be a sacrificial pawn in the service of their tireless and implacable mediocrity.

Parents protest at a college's 'A-level course in obscenity'

By JAMES MEIKLE
Education Reporter

A TORY MP is demanding an inquiry after teenagers were required to study an A-level text full of obscenities.

David Sumberg labelled a collection of poems by Tony Harrison as 'crude, obscene and offensive'.

Mr Sumberg, MP for Bury South, is to complain to Education Secretary Kenneth Baker.

He said: 'It goes to the root of what our children should be studying in preparation for their future lives.'

The Joint Matriculation Board, which is setting papers on works by the controversial poet for about 1,000 schoolchildren this summer, admitted it might have made a mistake.

The row comes two months after complaints over the Channel 4 screening of Harrison's recital of his poem v, which contains four-letter words.

Mr Roger Turner and his wife Joyce sent Mr Sumberg extracts from the volume their 16-year-old daughter

Tony Harrison: 'Family man'

Caroline was required to read at Bury College of Tertiary Education

Mrs Turner said Caroline was not due to take A-level this summer, and Harrison was not among the poets on next year's reading list.

College principal Tony Robinson, who claimed the poems had met with a 'positive response', said Mrs Turner could have suggested her daughter was withdrawn from the class.

Harrison's agent Gordon Dickerson said: 'He is a family man.

'He is regarded by his peers and others as one of the finest writers in the English language and uses the language in an exciting and articulate way.'

THURSDAY 14 JANUARY 1988

DAILY MAIL

78

Schools back poet

TEACHERS have defended "streetwise" poet Tony Harrison as they come under fire for teaching his "obscene" works.

Eleven schools in the region have an A-level syllabus which includes Harrison's controversial works. Many schools study the poet in other classes.

Tory MP David Sumberg has slammed the A-level text — Tony Harrison's Selected Poems — as "crude, obscene and offensive," and he has called for an inquiry into the poems being studied in school.

This comes two months after complaints at Harrison reciting his poem V, which contains four-letter words, on TV.

Mr Sumberg, MP for Bury South, said yesterday: 'I think it is the view of the majority of ordinary people that the poems are totally unacceptable as part of an A-level course."

But teachers who have chosen Harrison from a number of poets offered on the syllabus say youngsters in the region are "in tune" with the poet's North-East working class background and can more easily understand what he is saying.

Ian Mowbray, head of English at Washington School, said Harrison was a 'relevant and accessible poet' and said he was considering teaching his work.

He said: "Although his language is harsh, crude and forceful at times, he is also very moving." He said students saw him as someone from their working class environment who struggled with his academic potential.

Adrian Beard, head of English at Gosforth High School, has about 15 pupils who will be answering questions on Harrison on their A-level papers this summer. He said pupils identified with the things he was writing about.

He said people who found Harrison crude or obscene were those who looked out for dirty words and counted them up. "If naughty words are there, they are there for a poetic purpose," he added.

A spokesman for the Joint Matriculation Board, which is setting papers on works by the controversial poet said schools could choose Harrison from a number of poets on the syllabus.

Mr Harrison was unavailable for comment.

FRIDAY 15 JANUARY 1988
NORTHERN ECHO